Highlights of the Old Testament

Part 1: History
Genesis - Esther

A 13-Lesson Study Containing

Weekly Commentary

and

Daily Study Questions

Commentary by

Ray C. Stedman

Daily Study Questions by

Nancy J. Collins

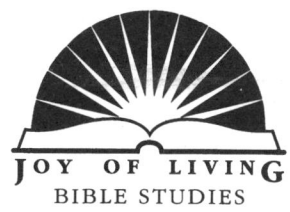

JOY OF LIVING
BIBLE STUDIES

Published by Joy of Living Bible Studies
Printed in U.S.A.

For a free catalog please contact us at:

800-999-2703 or 805-650-0838
website: www.joyofliving.org
e-mail: info@joyofliving.org

The commentary portion of these lessons was selected from Ray C. Stedman's sermons on "Highlights of the Bible: Overviews of the Old Testament Books of the Bible." (Sermons copyright 2010 by Ray Stedman Ministries; these sermons are the sole property of Ray Stedman Ministries, www.RayStedman.org.) Published by special arrangement with and permission of Ray Stedman Ministries.

ISBN   1-932017-62-3
        978-1-932017-62-5

About Joy of Living

For over 40 years Joy of Living has been effectively establishing individuals around the world in the sound, basic study of God's Word.

Evangelical and interdenominational, Joy of Living reaches across denominational and cultural barriers, enriching lives through the simple, pure truths of God's inspired Word, the Bible.

Studies are flexible, suited for both formal and informal meetings, as well as for personal study. Each lesson contains historical background, commentary, and a week's worth of personal application questions, leading readers to discover fresh insights into God's Word. Courses covering many books in both the Old and New Testaments are available. Selected courses are also available in several foreign languages. Contact the Joy of Living office for details.

Joy of Living Bible Studies was founded by Doris W. Greig in 1971 and has grown to include classes in nearly every state in the Union and many foreign countries.

Table of Contents

How to Use Joy of Living Materials

This unique Bible study series may be used by people who know nothing about the Bible, as well as by more knowledgeable Christians. Each person is nurtured and discipled in God's Word, and many develop a personal relationship with Jesus Christ as they study.

Joy of Living is based on the idea that each person needs to open the Bible and let God speak to them by His Holy Spirit, applying the Scripture's message to their needs and opportunities, their family, church, job, community, and the world at large.

Only a Bible is needed for this study series. While commentaries may be helpful, it is not recommended that people consult them as they work through the daily study questions. It is most important to allow the Holy Spirit to lead them through the Bible passage and apply it to their hearts and lives. If desired, additional commentaries may be consulted after answering the questions on a particular passage.

The first lesson of a series includes an introduction to the Bible book, plus the first week's daily study questions. Some questions are simple, and some are deeper for those who are more advanced. The individual works through the Bible passages each day, praying and asking God's guidance in applying the truth to their own life. (The next lesson will contain the commentary on the Bible passage being covered in the study questions.)

To Use in a Group Setting:

After the daily personal study of the passage has been completed, the class gathers in a small group, where they pray together and discuss what they have written in response to the questions about the passage, clarifying problem areas and getting more insight into the passage. The small group/discussion leader helps the group focus on biblical truth, and not just on personal problems. The student is the only person who sees their own answers and shares only what they feel comfortable sharing.

After small groups meet for discussion and prayer, they often gather in a large group meeting where a teacher gives a brief lecture covering the essential teaching of the Bible passage which was studied during the prior week and discussed in the small groups. The teacher may clarify the passage and challenge class members to live a more committed daily life.

At home, the student begins the next lesson, containing commentary notes on the prior week's passage and questions on a new Scripture passage.

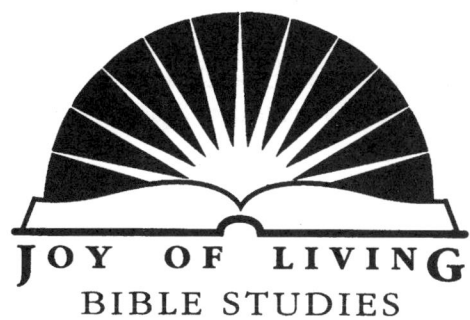

JOY OF LIVING
BIBLE STUDIES

Introduction

My cell phone is a marvelous tool, and on it reside many apps[1] for accomplishing various tasks. One of my favorites, when my husband and I travel, is the Maps app. Since he drives, and I am the navigator, I am constantly referring to my Maps app. Some people are content to use only its "turn by turn" instructions, but not me. I like to see the big picture—where I started, where I'm going, and where I am now according to the little blue dot. I frequently zoom in and out, using its "step by step"—or should I say "turn by turn"—directions, but also looking at the big picture. Each has its benefits.

So it is with God's Word. Most of the time when we read the Bible we are looking for the day by day instructions for living, which is good, but seeing and knowing God's Big Picture also has its benefits. The Big Picture lets us see how humanity got where it is today, helps us understand God a little better, reveals God's great plan for redeeming humanity, encourages us that everything is moving in accordance with that plan, and reveals our final destination.

In *Highlights of the Old Testament* we will take a brief look at each book of the Old Testament, and see what its overall message is, how it relates to the other books of the Bible, and what it reveals about God and His great plan.

No Other Book Like It

The Bible is easily the most fascinating book in the world. Granted it doesn't often appear as such to many. Some have thought it to be dry and even boring. But that is surely because they have not spent much time with it. It is a book of wonderful variety. There are beautiful love stories, which reflect the most tender and delicate of human passions. There are stories of political intrigue and maneuvering which rival anything we know today. There are stories of blood and thunder, which chill the heart. There are poetic passages, which soar to the very heights of ecstasy. There are narratives of intense interest and intricate plot, and there are strange and cryptic passages filled with weird symbols and allegories, which are difficult to penetrate and comprehend. From the Bible we can learn truths and proverbs for living and see history uncovered.

However, there is so much more to the Bible; there is no other book like it. Although it contains 66 books, recorded by forty men over a period of about 1600 years, the Bible has but one Author. Second Peter 1:21 tells us, "For prophecy never had its origin in the will of man, but men spoke from God as they were carried along by the Holy Spirit." And 2 Timothy 3:16 declares, "All Scripture is God-breathed." Bible teacher Henrietta Mears said, "The Bible is God's written revelation of His will to humanity. Its central theme is salvation through Jesus Christ."[2]

The Bible is divided into two major parts—the Old Testament and the New Testament. In the Old Testament we learn of the beginning of all things, including the fall of humanity and the entrance of sin and death into a perfect world. We also learn of the Savior that God promised would come. The New Testament tells us of Jesus Christ, who came to earth and who is that Savior.

In *Highlights of the Old Testament, Part 1,* we will cover the five Books of Law, also known as the Pentateuch, which include Genesis, Exodus, Leviticus, Numbers and Deuteronomy, and the twelve books of Old Testament history, which include Joshua, Judges, Ruth, 1 & 2 Samuel, 1 & 2 Kings, 1 & 2 Chronicles, Ezra, Nehemiah, and Esther. Throughout these Old Testament books God's holiness, God's righteousness, God's justice, God's mercy, and God's love are revealed. If your heart and mind are open, you will come to better know Him who loved us and sent His Son to save us.

A Daily Appointment with God

Make a daily appointment with God. Find a quiet spot. Take your Bible and your Bible study material with you. Remember how very important your appointment with God is, and make time to be with Him daily. Ask yourself the following things:

1. *How much time will I spend with the Lord each day?* Set a specific amount of time and write it on your calendar to set that time aside.

---

1. An "app" generally refers to a software program or application that you use online or on mobile devices.

2. Henrietta C. Mears. *What the Bible Is All About Bible Handbook, Revised and Updated* (Ventura: Regal, 2011) p13.

2. *What will I put aside in order to spend this time with the Lord?* Some examples might be watching television, texting, Tweeting, Facebook, or digital games. Each person will have to decide what his or her priorities are and what can be changed in their daily schedule to make time to spend with God.

3. *What is the best time for my appointment with God?* Consider whether you are a "morning" person or an "evening" person, and when you are least likely to be interrupted.

4. *Where is the quietest place for me to pray and study?* Look for both physical quiet and visual quiet—a place that won't constantly remind you of all the other things urgently awaiting your attention.

5. *Do I really want to spend time with God?* If your answer is "yes," God will bless you as you work out the details of how and when to do it. If your answer is "no," pray that God will give you a desire, a hunger to spend time with Him. He will do this for you!

Where Much of the Old Testament Took Place

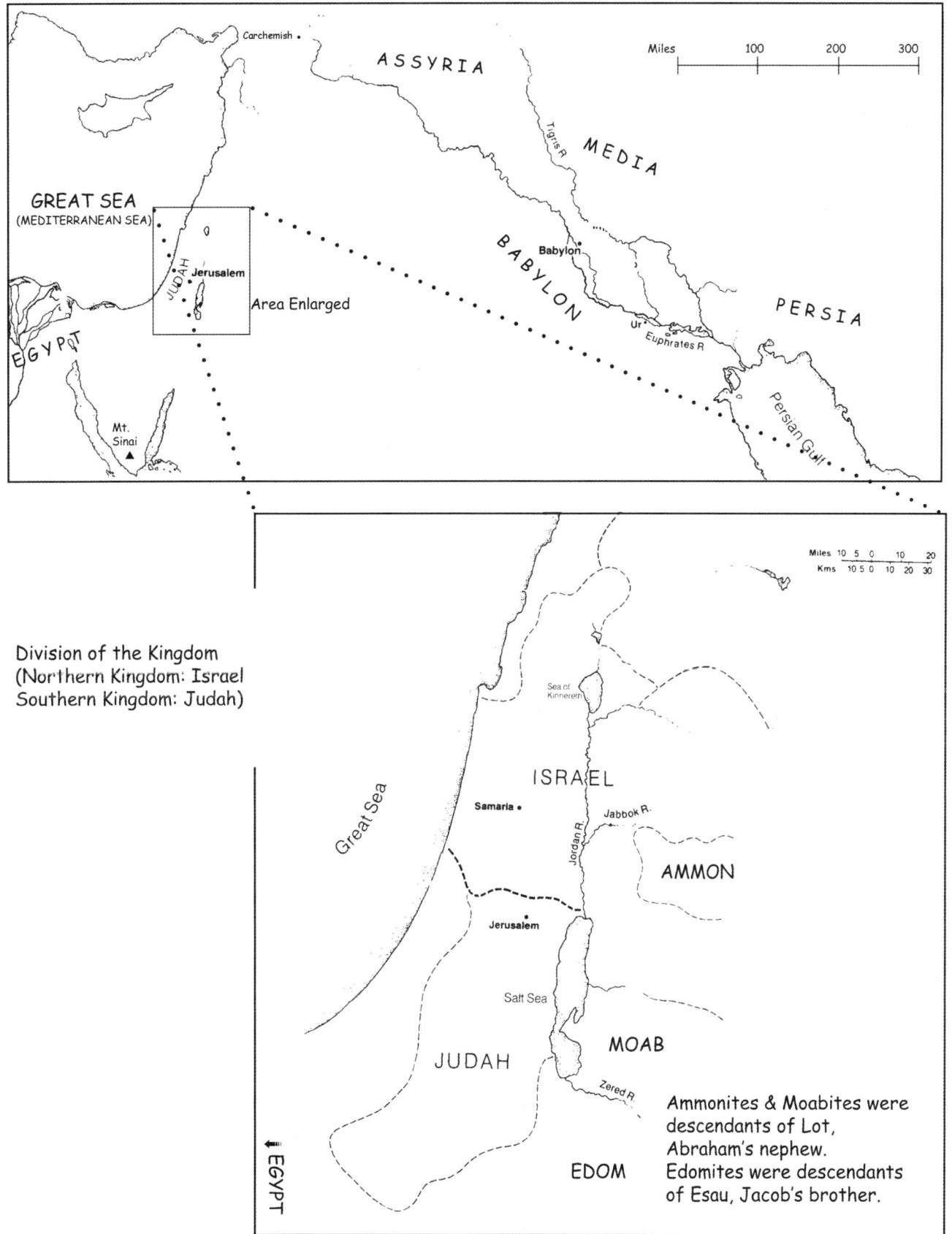

The Rulers of Israel and Judah

The United Kingdom of Israel and Judah

Saul	1050 - 1010 (41 years)
David	1010 - 970 (40 years)
Solomon	970 - 930 (40 years)

All dates are BC, and are based on *The NIV Study Bible*.[1]

The Southern Kingdom of Judah

Rehoboam	930 - 913 (17 years)
Abijah	913 - 910 (3 years)
Asa*	910 - 869 (41 years)

Jehoshaphat*	872 - 869 (co-regent with Asa - 4 years)
	869 - 848 (sole reign - 21 years)
Jehoram	848 - 841 (8 years)
Ahaziah	841 (1 year)
Athaliah	841 - 835 (7 years)
Joash*	835 - 796 (40 years)
Amaziah	796 - 792 (5 years)
	792 - 782 (prisoner of Jehoash of Israel - 10 years)
	782 - 767 (released / overlap with Azariah - 14 years)
Azariah	792 - 767 (overlap in reign with Amaziah - 24 years)
	767 - 740 (after Amaziah's death - 28 years)

Jotham	750 - 740 (co-regent with Azariah - 10 years)
	740 - 735 (sole reign - 6 years)
Ahaz	735 - 715 (16 years)
Hezekiah*	715 - 686 (29 years)
Manasseh	697 - 686 (co-regent with Hezekiah - 12 years)
	686 - 642 (sole reign - 43 years)
Amon	642 - 640 (2 years)
Josiah*	640 - 609 (31 years)
Johahaz	609 (3 months)
Jehoiakim	609 - 598 (11 years)
Jehoiachin	598 - 597 (3 months)
Zedekiah	597 - 586 (11 years)

Fall of the Southern Kingdom - 586

The Northern Kingdom of Israel

Jeroboam I	930 - 909 (22 years)
Nadab	909 - 908 (2 years)
Baasha	908 - 886 (24 years)
Elah	886 - 885 (2 years)
Zimri	885 (7 days)
Tibni	885 - 880 (ruled half of Israel - 6 years)
Omri	885 - 880 (ruled half of Israel - 6 years)
	880 - 874 (rulled all Israel - 6 years)
Ahab	874 - 853 (22 years)
Ahaziah	853 - 852 (2 years)
Joram	852 - 841 (12 years)
Jehu	841 - 814 (28 years)
Jehoahaz	814 - 798 (17 years)
Jehoash	798 - 782 (16 years)
Jeroboam II	793 - 782 (co-regent with Jehoash - 12 yrs)
	782 - 753 (sole reign - 29 years)
Zechariah	753 (6 months)
Shallum	752 (1 month)
Menahem	752 - 742 (ruled in Samaria - 10 years)
Pekahiah	742 - 740 (ruled in Samaria - 2 years)
Pekah	752 - 740 (ruled in Gilead - 12 years)
	740 - 732 (ruled over all Israel - 8 years)
Hoshea	732 - 722 (9 years)

Fall of the Northern Kingdom - 722

*In Judah, the southern kingdom, there were a few godly rulers among many who were evil. These godly rulers are marked with an asterik. In Israel, the northern kingdom, there were no godly rulers at all, but a continual succession of rulers who walked in idolatrous ways.

1. Kenneth Barker, editor. *The NIV Study Bible* (Grand Rapids: Zondervan, 1985). See charts: "Old & New Testament Chronology," "Rulers of Israel and Judah."

Study Questions

Before you begin your study this week:

- Pray and ask God to speak to you through His Holy Spirit.
- Use only the Bible for your answers.
- Write down your answers and the verses you used.
- Answer the "Challenge" questions if you have the time and want to do them.
- Share your answers to the "Personal" questions with the class only if you want to share them.

First Day: Read the Introduction to Highlights of the Old Testament, Part 1: History.

1. What meaningful or new thought did you find in the Introduction to *Highlights of the Old Testament, Part 1: History* or from your teacher's lecture? What personal application did you choose to apply to your life?

2. Look for a verse in the lesson to memorize this week. Write it down, carry it with you, tack it to your bulletin board, on the dashboard of your car, etc. Make a real effort to learn the verse and its "address" (reference of where it is found in the Bible).

3. This week's questions focus on Genesis 1-11. If you have time, you may want to read through the entire passage this week. As you answer the questions, you will be looking up passages of Scripture from various places in the Bible. This will help you discover that God's Word is a "whole," and that His message to us is the same from Genesis to Revelation.

Second Day:

Although we are studying Genesis 1-11 this week, today's questions will focus on the reliability and continuity of the Bible.

1. As we begin our study of the Bible, some of the first questions that may come to your mind are, "Who wrote the Bible?" and, "Is it reliable?" The Bible (Scripture) itself gives us these answers. Read 2 Timothy 3:16 and 2 Peter 1:21; then answer the following questions.

   a. Where did Scripture come from?

   b. I low did men receive the message?

   c. How much of Scripture is God-breathed?

2. Perhaps you wonder why there are so many opinions about what the Bible has to say, and if there is a way to know what God really means in the Bible. Read John 3:3-6; then answer the following questions.

   a. What must happen to a person before they can "see" or "perceive" the kingdom of God?

   b. What question does Nicodemus ask Jesus?

   c. What answer does Jesus give to Nicodemus?

3. Read 1 Corinthians 2:14 and answer the following questions.

   a. What does the person described here lack, so that he cannot accept the things of God?

   b. What does that person think of God's truth?

   c. Why can't that person understand God's truth?

4. a. Without being born of God's Spirit, a person can never understand the Bible or perceive God's truth. Read John 1:12-13. How is a person born of God?

    b. Personal: Have you been born of God's Spirit? If not, won't you confess that you are a sinner and receive Jesus as your Savior? He is the perfect Son of God who died to take the punishment for your sins. He rose on the third day, just as He predicted, to prove He has the power to offer you forgiveness and eternal life. (See Romans 6:23.) This is the starting point for knowing and understanding God. Write John 1:12-13 again, inserting your own name.

5. Personal: As you can see, Scripture itself declares that it is the Holy Spirit through the Word of God who reveals God's truth to us. Have you been one of those people who pick and choose what they want to believe? God does not give you that option. Either you believe what He says is true or you don't. If you have doubts, why not pray and ask Him to show you His truth as you continue in this study? If you already know His Word is true, write a prayer thanking Him for this assurance.

Third Day:

Genesis 1-2 tells the story of creation. Today's questions will help us discover more about creation and God's revelation of Himself.

1. Genesis is the first book of the Bible. It is the book of beginnings—of the world, the human race, sin in the world, the promise of redemption, family life, civilization, nations of the world, and the Hebrew race.[1] Read Genesis 1:1 and answer the following questions.

    a. With whom does the Bible begin?

    b. What action took place?

    c. When did this action happen?

2. Read Hebrews 1:1-3a. What do you learn about who created and sustains the world?

3. a. We marvel at the unending stars and the movement of the heavenly bodies. People have stood and gazed in awe and wonderment at this sight for centuries. What does Psalm 19:1 say about the skies and the heavens?

    b. Although the universe bears witness that there is an infinitely wise Creator, there are those who deny the existence of God. What does Psalm 14:1 say regarding those who say there is no God?

4. What does Romans 1:18-20 tell us about God, His creation and those who deny His existence?

5. A theory is "a supposition or a system of ideas intended to explain something."[2] Many so-called "truths" presented as facts are merely theories or suppositions, not actual facts. God has proven His existence and His nature to us by His creation. There are no proven facts of science that contradict what God has revealed to us in His Word. Read 1 Timothy 6:20-21. How should we handle any and all false knowledge?

6. Have you ever struggled to understand how God created everything? You may have questions that arise because of some "theory" you've heard. Stop and consider that people can only theorize, while God *knows*. He knows exactly what He did and how He did it. He tells us in the Bible what we need to know to begin, and allows us to search out and discover more about His creation. What are several things from God's creation that amaze you? Share with the class if you would like to.

---

1. *What the Bible Is All About Bible Handbook*, p34-35.
2. *New Oxford American Dictionary*

Fourth Day:

Genesis 2:7—3:21 tells us of the creation of humanity, and of God's early relationship with us.

1. a. Read Genesis 2:7. How did humanity come into existence?

   b. Read Genesis 5:1b-2. What additional information do you learn about humanity?

   c. Read Genesis 2:21-25 and describe the first human relationship.

   d. Read Genesis 4:1-2 and describe the first family unit.[1]

2. Although humanity was given the marriage relationship and the family unit, we will discover that Genesis reveals to us the inadequacy of people without God—that we can never discover or fulfill the true meaning of our lives without a genuine personal relationship with God. What do the following verses from the New Testament say regarding this?

   John 10:10b

   John 17:3

   1 John 5:20

3. a. Genesis chapter 3 tells the story of what disrupted humanity's relationship with God. Read Isaiah 59:2. What hinders our relationship with God?

   b. The penalty for sin is death—not just physical death, but eternal separation from God, who is life. Read Romans 5:12. How did sin and death enter the world? (You can read the full story about this in Genesis 3.)

4. What do the following verses say regarding God's remedy for this situation?

   1 Corinthians 15:3

   Colossians 1:19-22

   Romans 5:10

   Romans 10:9-10

5. Personal: Have you been reconciled to God and come into a relationship with Him by putting your faith in Jesus Christ to have your sins forgiven? If not, take a few moments now and pray, asking God to forgive you and trusting that Jesus' death on the cross paid the price for your sin. If you already have done this, write a short paragraph about when you accepted the Lord as your Savior.

---

1. Adam and Eve were the names of the first two people God created. All the rest of humanity descended from them.

Fifth Day:

In Genesis 4-7 we discover what happens when the fallen human nature is left unchecked.

1. Cain was the first-born child of Adam and Eve. Cain killed his brother Abel. (See Genesis 4:1-8.) From Genesis 4:25—5:4, what other children were born to Adam and Eve?

2. People increased on the face of the earth. Read Genesis 6:5,11-12 and describe the condition of humanity and the earth at this time.

3. Read Genesis 6:6-7. How did God feel about this, and what was He going to do?

4. There was, however, a man named Noah, who had three sons, Shem, Ham, and Japheth. From Genesis 6:8-9, describe Noah and his relationship with the Lord.

5. Read 2 Peter 2:5 and Hebrews 11:7. How did God wipe humanity from the face of the earth? What was the result of Noah's faith?

6. Personal: Noah was willing to stand for the Lord in the midst of an evil, ungodly society, and he was not silent about it. Do your life and the words that come from your mouth bear witness that you are a child of God?

Sixth Day:

Genesis 9-11 tells about the beginning of various people groups. Today's questions will help us understand where humanity is today.

1. After the flood, what command did God give to Noah and his sons in Genesis 9:1?

2. What was humanity's key unifying factor in Genesis 11:1?

3. In Genesis 11:2-5, we see that in direct disobedience to God's command to fill the earth, men built a tower in an effort to keep themselves from being scattered over the face of the earth. Why did God confuse their language? (Genesis 11:6-7)

4. What were the results of the confusion? (Genesis 11:8-9)

5. Thus, for humanity's sake, to keep us from destroying ourselves by ignorant ambition, God confused our language, and we were scattered over the face of the earth. What may appear to be a catastrophe in our eyes may actually be God's hand of grace and mercy. What does Isaiah 55:8-9 say regarding this?

6. Personal: Have you ever considered this truth before? Are you willing to trust God even when you don't understand why He has allowed something in your life? What situation are you facing right now that requires you to trust God?

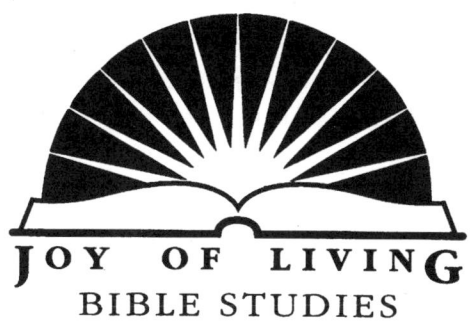

JOY OF LIVING
BIBLE STUDIES

Genesis 1-11 — The Beginnings of Humanity[1]

There are no writings more important for the proper understanding of history and humanity than the first chapters of Genesis. Here the secret of human sinfulness is revealed. In these opening chapters of the Bible is the first revelation of divine redemption and grace. Here the essential groundwork is laid for the understanding of the cross of Jesus Christ.

Genesis traces the story of humanity from its beginning within the natural world, and follows its history in a continually narrowing process down to the story of four great men of the past: Abraham, Isaac, Jacob, and Joseph. But Genesis is not only history; it is also a book with a single message: *humanity's need for God.* Genesis reveals that people can never be complete without God, that we can never discover or fulfill the true meaning of our lives without a genuine and personal relationship with God.

Humanity in the Universe

Genesis opens with the greatest material fact in all human life—that we are living in a universe. We are living on a planet shared with billions of other human beings, and our planet is part of a solar system. The whole solar system—the sun with all its planets—is making its way through a great whirling body of stars called a galaxy. This galaxy is moving at incredible speed through the vastness of space in conjunction with countless other galaxies.

It is precisely at that point that the Bible opens: "In the beginning God created the heavens and the earth" (Genesis 1:1). What a strange conjunction—to put all the vast heavens on one side and our tiny planet Earth on the other. But the book moves right on to tell us that humanity—insignificant humanity, we tiny specks of life living on a minor planet in the midst of this unthinkably vast universe—are the object of God's concern.

God has made the physical universe to reveal spiritual reality. The first truth God would suggest to us, manifested in the material universe all around us, is that there is a heavenly as well as an earthly life. There is a difference between the heavenly life of God and the earthly life of humanity. The supreme subject of the Bible will be how to move from the level of earth to the life of the heavens. This differ-

ence is declared by Isaiah, where God says, "For my thoughts are not your thoughts, neither are your ways my ways...As the heavens are higher than the earth, so are my ways higher than your ways and my thoughts than your thoughts" (Isaiah 55:8-9).

The Creation

We have seen that the greatest observable fact known to humanity is the existence of the universe. To this, Genesis 1:1 links the greatest fact made known by revelation—the existence of a God who creates. There is thus brought together at the beginning of the Bible a recognition of the two great sources of human knowledge—*nature*, discoverable by the five senses; and *revelation*, which is discoverable only by a mind and heart illuminated by the Spirit of God. Both of these sources of knowledge originate with God. Nature is designed to teach certain facts about God, but revelation is designed to bring us to the God about whom nature speaks.

Genesis 1:2 adds the information that the earth began as a planet covered by an uninterrupted ocean, which was itself wrapped in darkness. The revelation of Scripture says that the earth was "formless and empty." It was simply one great, vast deep of water covering the whole world, with no life in it. With that picture science fully agrees. But the revelation of Scripture is a key factor that many scientists do not acknowledge. Scripture's revelation says, "The Spirit of God was hovering over the waters." God was at work in His universe, interacting and interrelating with it.

The first step God took was to create light. Light is absolutely essential to life. With the advent of light we are now ready for the record of the six days of creation. How are we to view these days? Are they 24-hour days, constituting one literal week, or do they represent long and indefinite ages of time? It is my conviction that the controversy which has endlessly raged upon this question has been largely responsible for missing the real purpose for which God gives to us this first chapter of Genesis.

God was moving toward a goal, which He had clearly in mind from the beginning. The steps God took to accomplish this goal are recorded as several great creative acts, occurring in progressive stages, which logically succeed one another. It did not all happen at once. God did not bring the world and the universe into being with a snap of His fingers or with one sentence from His lips. He chose to do it in stages, which are very clearly evident throughout this passage.

---

1. This is an overview. You can study Genesis in more detail in the Joy of Living study titled *Genesis.*

Genesis 1 introduces in physical symbolism the great themes that will be amplified throughout the rest of the book. In other words, there are great lessons that God has deeply etched in nature in order to remind us of corresponding realities in our lives. Let us go through the creative days from this point of view, and we will see what I believe to be the real point of this passage.

Day 1: Light and Darkness

Day one describes the creation of light and and its separation from darkness. The light is said to be good and the darkness by definition is not good. Both these words, *light* and *darkness*, are used subsequently in Scripture to picture good and evil. Throughout our lives we will need to discern between good and evil, right and wrong, truth and error. We are reminded of this distiinction every day and night.

Day 2: The Expanse

On day two God created the "expanse" which separates the waters below from the waters above, and is called "sky." Physically this is a description of the creation of the atmosphere around the earth, which supports great quantities of water in evaporated form above the earth and separates it from the oceans below. This ocean and sky, divided asunder, picture for us the reality of human physical life and a subsequent heavenly life. Human existence is not over when this earthly life is over. The two levels of human existence are tied together with invisible but very real links, and one merges into the other just as oceans, by evaporation, move into the waters of the air.

People have forgotten these two facts, revealed in the first two creative days, and this is the root cause for the violence and moral decline of our day. We no longer seek to distinguish between good and evil, between light and darkness. It is also evident that we no longer want to think about the life to come. We want everything now. Instant happiness! But we must remember that this present earthly life is only a part of the whole; that eternity—and all the good things God has planned for us—is stretching before us; and that the choices we make now will determine our experience of eternity.

Day 3: Land and Plant Life

Day three was a double day in which there was first, the emergence of the land from the oceans, and second, the appearance of life upon the earth in the form of plants, trees and vegetation. The truth God wants us to learn from this is that there is an old, fallen humanity—represented by the oceans—which by nature is incapable of bringing forth what God desires, but there is also a new, redeemed humanity—the land—called out of the old, which will be capable of producing the fruit God envisions. In the second part of the third day that fruit actually appeared and was pronounced by God to be good. This fruit was a result of the activity of the Spirit upon the barren waters, just as He also brings forth fruit from the redeemed believer. (See John 3:3-6 and Galatians 5:19-23.)

Day 4: Sun, Moon and Stars

Day four brought the creation of the sun, moon, and stars, and the placing of them as lights and signs to govern the seasons of earth. The sun clearly pictures Jesus Himself (foretold in Malachi 4:2 as "the sun of righteousness") as the light of the world. The moon, reflecting the brightness of the sun and shining in the darkness of the night, is a symbol of the church, the body of Christ, shining in the moral darkness of this world. The stars are used repeatedly in Scripture as symbols of individuals who shine with great moral influence upon others.

Day 5: Sea Creatures and Birds

The fifth day brought the creation of birds flying in the expanse above the earth, and of every living creature that moves in the waters of the seas. Since the atmosphere above depicts the heavenly kind of life and the waters are a picture of unregenerate humanity, this day of creation symbolizes to us the possibility of living triumphantly in either an alien or a hostile environment. The spiritual life is alien to natural humanity, but by the redemption of God we can "soar on wings like eagles" (Isaiah 40:31). The world is a hostile environment to us, but we can learn to live in it as effectively as a fish learns to swim in the sea.

Day 6: Animals and Humanity

This sixth day was also a double day. During the first part of the day God created the land animals, followed by the creation of humanity. This is in exact accordance with the fossil records—people make their appearance last in the order of life. But there are some distinctive things said of us that are never said of any of the animal creation.

First, God held a divine consultation about humanity, saying, "Let us make man in our image, in our likeness" (Genesis 1:26). This divine conversation is the first hint given to us that God consists of more than one person.[1] This revelation is given only in connection with the emergence of people upon the earth.

The key fact about people is that we are made in the "image" and "likeness" of God. That image is found not in our body or in our personality, but in our *spirit*. For, as Jesus told the woman at the well in Samaria, "God is spirit, and his worshippers must worship in spirit and in truth" (John 4:24). But what is godlike about our spirit? If the spirit is made in the image of God, then it can do things that God can do but no animal can. Three things are suggested throughout Genesis 1 which God does: He creates; He communicates; and He evaluates, pronouncing some things good and others not good. Likewise, we can create, we can communicate, and we have a moral sense, recognizing some things as good and others as bad.

However, though people have retained the *image*, we have now lost the *likeness* of God. Image is the capacity to be God-like, but likeness is the proper functioning of that capacity. Adam not only had the ability to be creative, to communicate, to make moral choices—but he actually exercised the function of God-likeness. The secret, as we learn from the rest of Scripture, lay in an inner dependence on God that continually repudiated self-confidence.

Day 7: Rest

The seventh day was quite different from all the preceding six. There was no movement from incompleteness to completeness. It was, instead, a day characterized by rest; God ceased His labors,

---

1. The doctrine of the Trinity means that there is one God who eternally exists as three distinct Persons—the Father, Son, and Holy Spirit

intending it to be a picture of what is called later in Scripture the "rest" of faith. Hebrews 4:10 declares, "For anyone who enters God's rest also rests from his own work, just as God did from his."

Here is pictured the principle of human behavior by which God intends us to operate, and which was His intention from the very beginning of history. It is from this principle that people fell, and it is to this principle in Jesus Christ that we are to be restored. It is the principle of human activity resting upon an indwelling God to produce extraordinary results.

Man and Woman

Genesis chapter 2 finds the man walking in the Garden of Eden in communion with God. At this point, God gives him a research project—to investigate the animal world in search for a possible counterpart to himself. God knew that the man would not find what he was looking for, but in the process the man discovered at least four marvelous truths.

First, he learned that woman was not to be a mere beast of burden as the animals are, because that would not in any way fulfill his need for a helper and companion.

Second, woman was not to be merely a biological laboratory for the producing of children. This is what the animals use sex for, but that was not sufficient for Adam's needs. Human sex, therefore, is different from that among the animals.

Third, Adam learned that woman was not a thing outside himself—she is not something to be used at the whim of a man and then disposed of. She is to be a helper, fit for him, corresponding to him.

So, we are told that Adam fell into a deep sleep, and God took one of his ribs and from it made a woman and brought her to him. This period of Adam's unconsciousness strongly suggests that the relationship of marriage is far deeper than mere surface affection. It touches not only the conscious life, but the subconscious, even the unconscious as well.

Chapter 2 ends with a marvelous statement of the principles God intends for marriage:

- First, marriage involves a complete *identity* of the partners. The two are to become one. This is a growing process as a couple lives together, merging their lives both physically and emotionally, and creating a single history.

- The second principle is that of *headship,* which marks the role of the man as the leader in determining the direction in which a home should go, and the woman's responsibility to support and sustain that leadership.

- The third factor is that of *permanence*. Men and women are to be united to one another—he is to stay with her and she with him, because marriage is a permanent bond.

- The fourth factor is revealed in the verse, "The man and his wife were both naked, and they felt no shame" (Genesis 2:25). This speaks clearly of openness and free *communication.*

Humanity's Limitation

In chapter 3 of Genesis we find the explanation for the whole history of human heartache and misery. Remove this chapter from the Bible, and the rest of it is beyond explanation. But the most striking thing about it is that we find ourselves in this chapter. The temptation and the fall are reproduced in our lives many times a day. We have all heard the voice of the tempter and felt the drawing of sin, and we all know the pangs of guilt that follow.

It was clearly the devil, in his character as an angel of light, who confronted the woman in the Garden of Eden. His tactic with her was to arouse desire. First he implanted in her heart a distrust of God's love, "Did God really say, 'You must not eat from any tree in the garden'?" (Genesis 3:1). Next, he dared to deny openly the results that God had stated would occur, "You will not surely die," he said (Genesis 3:4). Then he clinched his attack with a distorted truth, "God knows that in the day you eat from it your eyes will be opened, and you will be like God, knowing good and evil" (Genesis 3:5).

The result was that Eve took the fruit and ate. But there was still hope for the human race. Adam had not yet fallen, only Eve. A battle had been lost, but not the war. In the innocent but ominous words, "She also gave some to her husband, who was with her, and he ate it" (Genesis 3:6), we face the beginning of the darkness of a fallen humanity. What the Bible calls "death" immediately followed.

The first sign of death at work in human life was that Adam and Eve knew they were naked. This was the birth of self-consciousness, and the immediate result was an attempt to cover up. The second mark of death was the tendency to hide. It revealed the fact of guilt—that inner torment we are all familiar with, which cannot be turned off no matter how hard we try. The third mark of death was the beginning of blame—the passing of the buck from Adam to Eve, and from Eve to the serpent. Behind both excuses was the unspoken suggestion that it was really God's fault. Thus they attempted to turn guilt into fate and make of themselves mere innocent victims suffering from a breakdown in creation for which God was responsible. The fourth mark of death was the divine establishment of the limits of life: pain, sweat and death. Adam and Eve must learn the hard cruel facts of life lived apart from an intimate relationship with God.

At this point, God clothed them with animal skins as a picture—as all animal sacrifices are—to teach us the great truth that ultimately it is God Himself who bears eternally the agony of our sin. This was followed by banishment from the Garden.

The Beginning of Human Society

In Genesis chapters 4-11, relating early human history, we also see the underlying threads of all human society for all time. Without doubt there was a real Cain, there was a genuine 40-day deluge, there was an ark made of cypress wood, and there was an actual tower of babbling confusion. There is no need to question the historicity of these events, but they are recorded to teach us graphically the principles on which humanity has built society and the inherent flaws in those principles.

History as we know it is the story of wars, battles, and the bloodshed of people. The key to this eternal struggle actually lies in the story that took place at the dawn of history—the story of two brothers: Cain and Abel. The focus of the story is in the two offerings which these brothers brought to God. Abel's offering of a lamb was accepted and Cain's offering of grain was rejected. Surely the commentators are right in indicating that God's reason for rejecting Cain's offering was that it was a bloodless offering, and therefore could not take away sin, for "without the shedding of blood there is no forgiveness" (Hebrews 9:22).[1]

Cain was angry at God's action, and when given opportunity to repent refused to do so. Thus, when he later found himself in the field with his brother Abel, Cain's jealousy took over, and Abel died, murdered by his brother's hand. Thus the roots of human warfare are seen to lie in the jealous and envious spirit in the heart, and in the ease with which we utter Cain's contemptuous words, "Am I my brother's keeper?" (Genesis 4:9).

The blood of Abel cried from the ground for justice, and God answered by placing a curse on Cain. The ground would no longer yield crops to him, and he would therefore be forced to wander from place to place. To protect Cain from excess punishment, God set a mark upon him. It was not a mark of shame, as many interpret it, but a mark of grace by which God was saying, "This man is still my property; he is guilty, he is a murderer, but he is still mine, and don't forget it."

The Expansion of Civilization

The next element traced in Genesis was the beginning of civilization. To Cain was born Enoch, who built a city. From the descriptions of Enoch's descendants, we see that within the city were found all the ingredients of modern life—travel, music and the arts, the use of metals, the organized political life, and the domestication of animals. Polygamy appeared with Lamech and his two wives. Violence and murder were justified on the grounds of self-defense.

But in the midst of this deterioration God had another plan already underway. Adam lay with his wife again, and she gave birth to a son and named him Seth. Through Seth's descendants the Savior of the world would come. Genesis 5 traces the beginning of this redemptive work of God. The focus of the chapter is Enoch, who learned to walk in fellowship with God in the midst of a godless and violent generation.

1. Although there is no record of God instructing Cain and Abel regarding the type of offering they were to bring, we know that God's message does not contradict itself. Surely His communication to Adam and Eve, Cain and Abel, was in harmony with what He says throughout the Bible. In Genesis 3 God covered Adam and Eve's nakedness—brought about by not believing and obeying God—by the shedding of the blood of an animal. This is the first record of the shedding of blood and it pointed to the coming Savior who would die for the sin of the world. All through the Old Testament communication and worship took place with the sacrifice of a lamb being presented.

God's Judgment

When "The Lord saw how great man's wickedness on the earth had become" (Genesis 6:5), God announced to Noah that He intended to judge the world, and He commanded Noah to build an ark of safety which would be his means of deliverance from the coming catastrophe. When the ark was completed, Noah was invited to enter it with all his family, also bringing two of every kind of animal and seven of clean animals. Noah demonstrated his faith by building and entering the ark in obedience to the word of God, against the ridicule and contempt of his contemporaries.

So the flood came. The whole earth was covered to the tops of the mountains and all life perished except the handful of humans and animals in the ark, and those marine animals which could survive in the waters. The rain continued for 40 days and nights and then ceased. After 150 days the waters began to abate, and on the seventeenth day of the seventh month the ark came to rest on the mountains of Ararat. The emergence of Noah from the ark is intended to be a picture of the new beginning of life which every Christian experiences when he enters into the resurrection life of Jesus Christ by the new birth.

God's Intervention

Chapter 9 of Genesis records a covenant made with Noah, but also with all humanity. This covenant contained God's provision for the ordering of human life. First, nature was made to be dependable, secured by the promise of the rainbow from universal catastrophe. Second, humanity's rule over the animal world through fear was disclosed, and animals were given to people as food, along with plant life. Third, human life was seen to be so sacred that only God had the right to take it, except in the case of a murderer, in which case God used the organized system of government as His instrument (see Romans 13:3-4). Thus a foundation was laid for police work and capital punishment. Fourth, the command was given, once again, to multiply and populate the earth.

Genesis 10 continues the narrative of the flood, giving us an account of the offspring of Noah's sons, the nations that sprang from them and the general location where they settled. Genesis 11 gives the detailed account of how this dispersion of the nations came about. All people had one language. As they moved eastward they settled in the land of Shinar or Babylonia. They soon discovered they could invent their own materials for building, and they were fired with desire to build two things—a city and a tower—to keep from being scattered over the face of the whole earth, in direct contrast to God's command to populate the earth.

God took note of their unity and their creativity and stated, "Nothing they plan to do will be impossible for them" (Genesis 11:6). For humanity's sake, to keep them from destroying themselves by ignorant ambition, God confused their language, and people were scattered over the face of the earth. Thus the atmosphere of this time became one of movement and migration—people thrusting out from the center like spokes of a wheel radiating out into the corners of the earth.

Study Questions

Before you begin your study this week:

- 🙠 Pray and ask God to speak to you through His Holy Spirit.
- 🙠 Use only the Bible for your answers.
- 🙠 Write down your answers and the verses you used.
- 🙠 Answer the "Challenge" questions if you have the time and want to do them.
- 🙠 Share your answers to the "Personal" questions with the class only if you want to share them.

First Day: Read the Commentary on Genesis 1-11.

1. What meaningful or new thought did you find in the commentary on Genesis 1-11 or from your teacher's lecture? What personal application did you choose to apply to your life?

2. Look for a verse in the lesson to memorize this week. Write it down, carry it with you, tack it to your bulletin board, on the dashboard of your car, etc. Make a real effort to learn the verse and its "address" (reference of where it is found in the Bible).

3. This week's questions focus on Genesis 12-50. If you have time, you may want to read through the entire passage this week. As you answer the questions, you will be looking up passages of Scripture from various places in the Bible. This will help you discover that God's Word is a "whole," and that His message to us is the same from Genesis to Revelation.

Second Day:

In Genesis 1-11 we learned of the creation and the fall of the human race. In chapters 12-50 we will see the beginning of God's plan to redeem humanity: the call of one man, Abraham, from whose offspring the Savior—Jesus Christ—would come (see Romans 9:5). In this lesson we will discover what it takes to please God, and we will see that quality in action.

1. a. Summarize God's promise to Abraham (Abram) in Genesis 12:1-3. (You can read the entire story of Abraham in Genesis 11:26—25:10.)

   b. Read Hebrews 11:8. How was Abraham able to be obedient to this call from God?

2. Read Hebrews 11:11-12 (the full story is in Genesis 17-21). What problem did Abraham and Sarah have? Summarize the blessing God gave to them despite this seemingly insurmountable obstacle.

3. Read Hebrews 11:17-19 (the full story is in Genesis 22). How was Abraham tested, and what did he believe God would do?

4. Read Galatians 3:8-9, 16, 22, and 26, and summarize what God did for humanity through Abraham. What is the key element a person must have in order to partake of these promises?

5. Personal: As we see above, we become children of God by faith in Jesus Christ, who is the fulfillment of God's promise to Abraham. Read and summarize Romans 5:8-9 and 1 Corinthians 15:3-4. What does this mean to you personally?

Third Day:

1. Isaac was the child promised to Abraham through whom the promised blessings would be fulfilled (see Romans 9:7-9). You can read Isaac's complete story in Genesis 17:19—35:29. Isaac shared in the faith of his father Abraham. What promise did God give to Isaac in Genesis 26:2-4? How does this compare to the blessing given to Abraham in Genesis 12:1-3?

2. Read Hebrews 11:20 (the full story is in Genesis 27). How was Isaac able to bless his sons, Jacob and Esau, regarding God's promises for their future?

3. What promise did God give to Jacob in Genesis 28:10-14? How did this compare to the promises God gave to Abraham and then to Isaac?

4. Although Jacob was a schemer and thought he could live by his own efforts, God, in His grace, brought Jacob to a place where he finally gave up and trusted Him. God changed his name from Jacob to Israel (see Genesis 32:28).[1] Jacob continued to live by faith. What do you learn about this in Hebrews 11:21? (Jacob's full story is in Genesis 25-49.)

5. a. Each of these men, Abraham, Isaac, and Jacob, are commended for their faith in Hebrews 11. They believed God's promises to them and lived accordingly. What do you learn about faith from Hebrews 11:6?

   b. Read Jeremiah 29:13. What will be the result of seeking God earnestly and with all our heart?

6. Personal: What is your current relationship with God? Are you satisfied with your relationship with Him? What are you doing about it?

1. Jacob means "he grasps the heel" or "he deceives," and Israel means "he struggles with God." (*The NIV Study Bible*. See text notes on Genesis 25:26, 32:28.)

Fourth Day:

1. a. Joseph was one of Jacob's twelve sons. How did Jacob (Israel) feel about Joseph and why? (Genesis 37:3a)

   b. From Genesis 37:3b how did he show his partiality?

2. How did Joseph's brothers feel about this? (Genesis 37:4)

3. Read Genesis 37:28,36. As a result of his brothers' envy, what eventually happened to Joseph, and where did he end up?

4. a. Jacob was a man who loved God and had faith in Him. His sons were the forefathers of the twelve tribes of Israel. But none of them were perfect. Jacob showed favoritism. What does James 2:9 say about favoritism?

   b. The brothers were envious. What does James 3:16 say regarding envy?

5. a. The fact that a person loves and believes God does not mean he or she is perfect. What does Romans 3:23 say regarding this?

   b. What problem does this create for every person, and what is God's remedy?

   c. Personal: If you have not yet accepted this gift, won't you do it right now?

6. Personal: When we come to God by way of Jesus Christ, He doesn't just forgive our sins, but He also begins to change us to become like Himself (see Romans 8:29). What difference does this make to you?

Fifth Day:

1. a. Joseph went through many difficult trials in his life. (You can read his full story in Genesis 30:22—50:26.) Read Acts 7:9-10a. Who was with Joseph in Egypt and rescued him from his troubles?

   b. From Acts 7:10b, what did God give to Joseph, and what did He enable him to do? What was the result?

2. From Acts 7:11-12, what brought Joseph's brothers (referred to here as "our fathers") to Egypt?

3. From Acts 7:13-14, summarize how Jacob and his entire family ended up in Egypt.

4. Read Genesis 45:9-11 and describe what Joseph did for his father, his brothers, and their families.

5. God used Joseph to save his entire extended family, and thus saved the nation through whom the Savior would come. What truth does Joseph share in Genesis 50:20 that can encourage us when people do wrong to us?

6. Personal: Romans 8:28 expresses the same truth. In what ways does this change your attitude toward the situations in your life?

Sixth Day:

We have learned that Genesis is the beginning of God's revelation of Himself to humanity. There are those who say that since there is only one God, all the religions of the earth worship Him, each in their own way. According to the Bible this is not true.

1. Read Exodus 3:15. How does God refer to Himself? How long is He to be known this way?

2. What does Deuteronomy 4:39 say regarding the Lord?

3. Read John 14:6. What did Jesus say regarding our relationship with God the Father?

4. Personal: Have you ever had a discussion with someone about these things? Perhaps you have also believed that all religions worship the same deity. How has God's Word changed your understanding?

5. Personal: Describe in your own words what you've learned in the overview of Genesis. What difference it is making in your life?

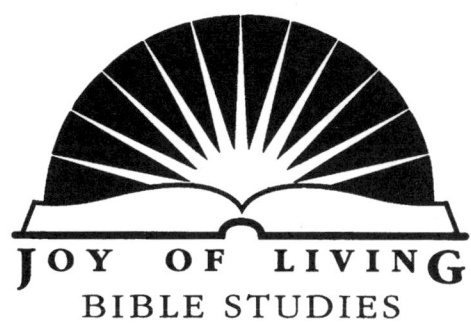

Genesis 12-50 — Narrowing the Focus[1]

In our previous lesson we ended with humanity thrusting out from the city of Babel, from which God had scattered them like spokes of a wheel radiating out into the corners of the earth. As humanity scatters, the narration of the Bible narrows and focuses on the man through whom the Savior of the world would come.

Abraham, Called by God (Genesis 12-25)

Abraham (called Abram until God changed his name to Abraham), a descendant of Seth through Noah and then Shem, was human like the rest of us. It was not Abraham's righteousness that drew God to him. It was God's call and His grace that drew Abraham to God.

Abraham's life exemplifies the process of achieving righteousness by faith. God appeared and conversed with Abraham on many occasions. Called "God's friend" in James 2:23, Abraham depicts forever the friendship which God desires to have in intimate communion with everyone who is made righteous by faith. Abraham learned seven lessons of faith, which are paralleled in the life of every believer today.

1. Obedience (Genesis 12:1-8)

It is not faith to simply say, "I believe." It is necessary to add, "I obey." This is "obedience that comes from faith" (Romans 1:5). In his first encounter with God Abraham was sent out to an unknown destination, but with the promise that God would go with him and show him the way. He was told that if he was obedient, God would make him into a great nation, bless him, and make his name great, and that all peoples on earth would be blessed through him. Through this promise we see another hint of God's eternal plan—the plan to send a Savior to redeem humanity.

Though Abraham was 75 years old, his obedience was immediate. He left Ur and went to Haran. Then, after his father Terah's death, Abraham went to the land of Canaan. The parallel in today's believers is found in a willingness to turn from the natural claims of family and friends, and to recognize the right of God to lead and direct our lives.

In Canaan God again appeared to Abraham, promising to give the land to his offspring, despite its present possession by Canaanite tribes. Abraham's life in the land is characterized by two symbols: a tent and an altar. The tent is the symbol of the pilgrim character of his

existence. He is never to own the land outright, but is to be a sojourner in it. The altar is the symbol of communion with a living God. It is the secret of the ability to endure in a land possessed by enemies. Every believer should remember that this world is not our home, and that we are merely passing through (see Hebrews 11:13; 1 Peter 1:1; 2:11). We must set our hearts on those things that are eternal. And we must have an altar—a personal time alone with God for Bible reading and prayer—so that we can endure in a hostile world.

2. Sufficiency (Genesis 12:9-20)

The second lesson Abraham learned was the *sufficiency of God to meet all human need*. Abraham's faith was tested by a famine in the land. He trusted God enough not to return to Haran, but he did flee the famine by going down to Egypt. His weak faith led Abraham to resort to a lie to protect himself from harm, and he then found himself a recipient of Pharaoh's rebuke. Thus, through failure, Abraham learned the necessary truth: God was able to supply his need, even in the midst of pressure and circumstantial difficulty. God has not changed. He will supply the need of each of His children (see Philippians 4:19).

3. Humility (Genesis 13)

When a dispute arose between the herdsmen of Abraham and of his nephew Lot over the use of the land, even though Abraham was the older and had the God-given right of first choice, he exhibited the humility of faith and allowed Lot to choose first. Abraham had learned to trust God to provide for him. Lot chose his land on the basis of selfishness and greed, choosing what appeared to be the best, and ended up in Sodom. Even though Lot chose his portion of the land, he did not truly possess it, because God gave Abraham all the land, including that which Lot had chosen for himself. We see that God's children are called to risk the obedience of faith, believing that God will take care of them even though they apparently are giving up their rights.

4. Boldness (Genesis 14:1-16)

When five kings from the east invaded the valley of the Dead Sea, Lot was captured. Though greatly outnumbered, Abraham gathered his servants about him, and with a company of 318 he pursued the united armies and overcame them in a great battle. Abraham had learned that it is God who gives the victory.

5. Independence From Human Resources (Genesis 14:17—15:21)

On Abraham's triumphant return he was met by Melchizedek at the King's Valley. Melchizedek appeared as the picture of an eternal priesthood, to bless Abraham and remind him that it was God who

---

1. This is an overview. You can study Genesis in more detail in the Joy of Living study titled *Genesis*.

gave him the victory. Abraham honored God by giving a tenth of everything to Melchizedek. Likewise, believers are to honor God with our wealth and with the firstfruits of all that we receive (see Proverbs 3:9). Abraham was also met by the King of Sodom, who offered to make him rich. Abraham refused to be made rich except by God Himself.

The Lord declared that He was Abraham's shield for his protection and his very great reward. Nothing is of greater worth than knowing and having a relationship with God. God then promised Abraham an heir from his own bloodline, from whom would come offspring as numerous as the stars of the sky. Despite his age, Abraham believed in the promise of a coming son, and for the first time in Scripture we read the great sentence, "Abram believed the Lord, and he credited it to him as righteousness" (Genesis 15:6).

6. Endurance and Patience (Genesis 16-20)

After 12 years of waiting for God to fulfill His promise of a son, Sarah (called Sarai until God changed her name to Sarah) and Abraham resorted to a human plan to "help God along." Hagar, Sarah's maid, was given to Abraham as a wife, and from her was born Ishmael. Abraham reaped the harvest of his folly in the continual strife between Sarah and Hagar, and the eventual exclusion of Hagar from the household.

God then appeared to Abraham again, and an everlasting covenant was made, symbolized by the change of names from Abram (exalted father) to Abraham (the father of many) and from Sarai to Sarah (princess). In this covenant God promised Abraham that he will be the father of many nations, that kings will come from him, that the whole land of Canaan will be given to him and his descendants as an everlasting possession, and that God Himself will be their God. This was confirmed by a new revelation of God's name, El Shaddai, which means "the God who is sufficient." The sign of this new covenant was circumcision, the outward sign of an invisible inward truth.

Genesis 17 records another appearance of God to Abraham. Three strangers appeared to him as he sat in the door of his tent. As he showed them hospitality, there gradually dawned upon him the realization that it was the Lord Himself, accompanied by two angels. Sarah, listening behind the tent door, heard the announcement that she would bear a son within a year, and laughed. But God graciously met her with a divine revelation upon which her faith might rest. He asked, "Is anything too hard for the Lord?" (Genesis 18:14).

Then God revealed to Abraham the imminent destruction of the cities of the plain for their extreme wickedness and unbelief. With obvious reverence, Abraham interceded with God on behalf of the doomed cities, based upon his awareness of the character of God: "Will not the Judge of all the earth do right?" (Genesis 18:25). It would be a mistake to view Abraham's prayers as reflecting more mercy than does God. We learn from the New Testament that it is the Spirit of God who prays within the believer, urging him to the specific requests that are made (see Romans 8:26). Thus it was God's mercy, expressed through Abraham's prayers, that limited and tempered the justice and wrath of God. God goes beyond anything we ask. Abraham stopped at ten righteous persons, but God saved the few in whom there was any recogni-

tion of Himself. Genesis 19 records the two angels' visit to Sodom and Gomorrah. Lot himself was righteous, as the New Testament makes clear (see 2 Peter 2:7), but his righteousness had been compromised by his conformity to Sodom's ways, and he found himself unable to influence his city, or even his family, toward righteousness.

Again we see a weakness in Abraham's faith in Genesis 20. Surrounded by the men of Gerar, Abraham again lied concerning his wife Sarah. Once again a heathen king rebuked him for his lack of complete honesty. These deflections in Abraham's faith illustrate for us how easy it is to take our eyes off the Lord and to make decisions and take action without putting our confidence and trust in the living God.

At long last Sarah's laugh of incredulity was turned into the laughter of realization. As Isaac, the child of promise, grew, problems developed with Ishmael. Eventually Abraham, in simple obedience to God's direction, sent forth Hagar and Ishmael. God promised to provide for Hagar and her son, but they would not inherit what was to be given to the offspring of Abraham and Sarah. It was through their son Isaac that God's promises would be fulfilled and the Savior of the world would come.

7. Intimacy with God (Genesis 22:1—25:18)

Chapter 22 records the last appearance of God to Abraham. Isaac had grown to young manhood. God asked that Isaac, as the pride of his father's heart, be offered as a sacrifice to Him whom Abraham served. It was Abraham's greatest test. But faith enabled him to triumph as he rested upon his intimate knowledge of the character of God and knew that God was able even to raise his son from death (see Hebrews 11:17-19). As we develop an intimacy with God and come to know and trust His character, we can have confidence and peace throughout whatever trials we face.

Chapter 23 records Sarah's death and Abraham's sorrow. For her burial Abraham purchased the cave of Machpelah from the Hittites. Thus Abraham's first actual possession in the land was a grave.

Chapter 24 tells the story of Abraham's servant Eliezer, sent to find a bride for Isaac. Running throughout the account is the theme of the sovereign call of God. This accounts for Rebecca's willingness to leave her home and family to join a man she had never seen, in a land to which she had never been. Abraham's faith was rewarded by seeing the union of his son with a woman of his own kindred, who, though they were of two different temperaments, would walk together in fulfillment of the divine purpose.

At the age of 175 Abraham died and was buried by his sons in the cave of Machpelah beside Sarah. Throughout the rest of the Bible, the figure of Abraham looms as a man of faith. By his experiences with God, and even by his failures, he has been taught the lessons of righteousness which come by faith alone.

Isaac, Heir of Promise (Genesis 25-36)

Isaac symbolizes the condition of those who are the sons of God by faith in Jesus Christ. He dwelt in the land in the midst of God's blessing, and was refreshed by a continual supply of water from the wells that he dug in various locations, despite the opposition of his enemies. After Abraham's death Isaac became the heir of God's promises to Abraham and of the blessings of God. But Isaac also reflected the weaknesses of his father. For in the land of Gerar he repeated his father's sin—out of fear he lied about his wife, and was rebuked by a man of the world. Although he received God's blessing and promises because he was Abraham's son, this didn't automatically make him the man of faith his father was.

When Isaac was an old man, he called his sons before him to give them his blessing. Before his twin sons Jacob and Esau were born, God told their mother Rebekah that the elder would serve the younger. Whether or not Isaac was aware of this we don't really know. We do know that when the sons appeared for their blessing, Isaac intended to give the greater blessing to Esau, the firstborn. Through a series of deceptions, masterminded by Rebekah, Jacob appeared before his blind father in the guise of Esau, and received the blessing of the firstborn. When Isaac found out that he had been tricked, he dared not alter the blessing he had pronounced, a fact he confirmed to Esau. God would have accomplished His purpose without Rebekah's deception (see Proverbs 19:21). Although God fulfilled His purpose for Jacob, both he and his mother reaped negative consequences for their sin.

Jacob, Deceiver and Deceived (Genesis 27-31)

Jacob's sin did not stop God's call and blessing to him. Likewise, our sinfulness does not stop God's call and blessing in our lives. Romans 5:8 says, "While we were still sinners, Christ died for us." God's plan for Jacob's life would be fulfilled. And just as God continues the work He began in us who believe, so God would begin and continue to work in Jacob throughout his life.

Esau held a grudge against Jacob because of his deception in obtaining the blessing and planned to kill him as soon as their father Isaac died. Rebekah, fearing what Esau would do, convinced Isaac to send Jacob far away to Laban, her brother, to find a wife.

On the first night of Jacob's journey, God appeared to him in a dream and extended and confirmed the promises to Jacob which He had first made to Abraham and then to Isaac. Jacob had thought he was alone and uncared for, but he found that God was with him and would continue to be with him, to help him and to bring him back to the land. In response, Jacob erected a stone, anointing it with oil, and named it Bethel. To this place Jacob returned again and again during his lifetime, gaining from each visit a renewed awareness of God's faithful love and sure promise. In the same way, each believer today must return again and again to the faithful promises of God and to the reminders of His love and care for us.

When Jacob arrived in Haran, he fell in love with Rachel at first sight. Having been welcomed into Laban's family, he must have felt that all was working out well, for he was promised Rachel for his wife after seven years of service to his uncle. But Jacob had to learn the harvest of deceit, and at the end of seven years he found himself tricked into marrying Leah, Laban's older daughter, instead of Rachel.

When Jacob protested, Laban offered to let him have Rachel, too, for yet another seven years' servitude. So great was Jacob's love, he consented to this. During this time a total of eleven sons were born to Jacob's wives and their handmaids who became his concubines. When Rachel gave birth to a son after many years of barrenness she named him Joseph. At that point Jacob decided that he should return to Canaan.

But God was not yet through with Jacob's training. He again experienced the deceitfulness of his uncle. Jacob had agreed to work for Laban for yet another seven years in return for flock of his own. In spite of Laban's ever changing agreement and Jacob's attempt to manipulate the circumstances, God's blessing resulted in a spectacular increase in Jacob's flocks during those years.

Once again God appeared to Jacob in a dream. He commanded him to return to the land of promise. To escape from Laban's wiles, Jacob left in the middle of the night with his wives, children, and flocks. Though Laban pursued him and caught up with him, God intervened and kept him from harming Jacob. Jacob and Laban then made a covenant of peace with one another, and Laban returned to his own home.

Twenty years of servitude had passed. During that time, in spite of Laban's trickery, God had taken Jacob from a lonely fugitive with no resources to an affluent herdsman with wives and children. But Jacob had not yet learned total dependence on God. That would happen only after he had wrestled with God and his human strength was broken completely.

Jacob, Man of God (Genesis 32-36)

Jacob traveled on toward home and his brother Esau, whom he had cheated so many years before. When Jacob learned that Esau was on his way to meet him with 400 armed men, he was in great fear and distress. Humbled at last, he sought the Lord, acknowledging his unworthiness and God's faithfulness to him. He then made plans to appease the wrath of Esau with gifts before they met in person. While Jacob waited alone, the angel of the Lord, in the form of a man, wrestled with him through the long night. As day broke the angel sought to disengage himself, but Jacob clung with stubborn persistence. The angel touched Jacob's hip and threw it out of joint, but still Jacob refused to let go until he was blessed of God. Then the divine being changed the name of Jacob to Israel, which means "he who prevails with God." As the sun rose, Jacob, a changed man, limped off to meet Esau. He no longer feared people, but was confident that God would fight his battles for him. When Esau arrived, his own heart had been strangely altered, and instead of attacking he embraced Jacob. Jacob was beginning to understand that God was his strength and refuge and was fully capable of working out all problems with which he might be confronted.

God appeared again to Jacob and sent him back to Bethel. There God renewed His promises to Jacob, and there Jacob's beloved wife Rachel gave birth to her second son Benjamin and died in childbirth.

Jacob traveled on to Mamre, where he found his aged father on his deathbed. He and Esau buried Isaac with honor and reverence.

Joseph, the Forerunner (Genesis 37-50)

The story of Joseph reveals yet another step in God's redemptive plan. Joseph appears as the forerunner, sent into Egypt to prepare the way for the coming of Jacob's family into that land. There they would eventually become the nation of Israel, to whom God would give His laws and reveal his standard of righteousness, and through whom He would send the Savior of the world.

We discover Joseph at the age of 17 working as a shepherd in his father's home in Hebron. Joseph was the obvious favorite of his father Jacob, who had bestowed on him a princely robe as a special mark of his favor. Therefore, he was the object of bitter hatred by his brothers. When, further, they learned that God had given Joseph two special dreams which predicted his elevation above his brothers, their hatred took a murderous form, and they sought a way to kill him.

When Jacob's sons delayed returning from Shechem where they were feeding their flocks, Jacob sent Joseph to check on his brothers. Seeing him coming from afar and recognizing the hated coat, his brothers plotted together to kill him, throw him into a pit, and tell their father that a wild beast had destroyed him. The oldest of the twelve, Reuben, objected and persuaded them to leave Joseph to die in the pit. While they prepared for their journey home, they saw a caravan of Ishmaelites traveling by and hit upon a scheme to sell Joseph to them as a slave, but to tell their father that he had been killed. Then they brought his coat, dipped in goat's blood, back to their father with the report that Joseph must have been killed by a wild beast. Jacob, who had deceived his own father Isaac, was now deceived by his sons.

Joseph was sold to Potiphar, an officer in the army of Egypt. The excellence of Joseph's character soon elevated him to a place of trust and responsibility, and he was put over all of Potiphar's household. Because Joseph was handsome and well-built, Potiphar's wife attempted to seduce him, but Joseph resisted. One day she found him alone and caught him by his cloak, attempting to drag him into her bed. Joseph fled from her presence, leaving his cloak behind. Potiphar's wife reported the incident to her husband as though Joseph had attempted to assault her, and Potiphar put Joseph in prison.

In all this there is no hint of bitterness or resentment on Joseph's part, but a quiet trust in God. Joseph's kindliness and skill soon won him a position in charge of the other prisoners. Once again, dreams played a large part in Joseph's story. This time Pharaoh's butler and baker, who were also in prison, were the dreamers, and Joseph was the interpreter. The dreams were fulfilled as Joseph said. The baker went to his death and the butler was restored to Pharaoh's household, but soon forgot his promise to remember Joseph when he was released. But another dream got Joseph out of prison two years later.

Pharaoh had a dream. He commanded his wise men to interpret the dream for him. When they could not, the chief butler remembered Joseph and told Pharaoh of his interpretative skill. Joseph was hast-

ily hauled from the dungeon and brought before Pharaoh. There he interpreted Pharaoh's dream, predicting seven years of good harvest followed by seven years of drought and famine. Pharaoh, impressed not only by Joseph's interpretative skills, but also by the wisdom with which he suggested ways to meet the coming crises, made Joseph the second-in-command of the kingdom.

Back in Canaan, Jacob and his sons were experiencing terrible famine. Jacob sent all his sons but Benjamin, the youngest, into Egypt to buy grain. When the brothers came before Joseph, he recognized them immediately, but did not reveal his knowledge. Instead he treated them roughly and accused them as spies come into the land. When they protested, he ordered that they leave one of the brothers behind as a hostage, return to Canaan, and bring back Benjamin as proof of their integrity. Simeon, the second oldest, remained behind, and the brothers returned to Canaan. Jacob at first was adamant that he would not let Benjamin leave. But the famine forced him to relent.

When the brothers returned to Egypt, Joseph entertained them in his own home, much to their bafflement and uncertainty. When they left, he commanded that the money they used to buy the grain be put back in their bags, and his own private cup be hidden in Benjamin's bag. Then he sent his servants after them to accuse them of stealing the cup. Protesting their innocence, they vowed that the man in whose bag the cup should be found would immediately be put to death. But when the cup was found in Benjamin's bag, they were overcome with sorrow, and were brought back to Joseph's presence.

There, in a most moving plea, Judah privately recited the whole story in Joseph's ear and begged of him that Joseph would permit him (Judah) to remain as hostage and let Benjamin go. Upon hearing this Joseph could not control himself any longer, and ordering all the Egyptians from the room, he made himself known to his brothers. The astonished brothers returned to Canaan with the good news, and Jacob was persuaded to come with them into Egypt.

As the aged Jacob neared his death, Joseph brought his two sons Manasseh and Ephraim before him to be blessed of him. When the old patriarch blessed them, he crossed his hands so that the blessing of the firstborn fell upon Ephraim, the younger, and Manasseh, the elder, was given the secondary blessing. Once again the right of the firstborn was transferred to the younger son. It was God's reminder that the right of the firstborn, which belonged to Adam, was now transferred to the last Adam (Jesus), that He might be "the firstborn over all creation" (Colossians 1:15).

The final chapter recounts how Joseph took the body of his father, Jacob, out of Egypt to Canaan and buried him with Abraham. Joseph then returned to Egypt where he lived till the age of 110 and died. Thus Genesis, which began with the creation of the heavens and the earth, ends in a coffin in Egypt. But behind the sad reality there burns the bright promise of God that a Savior would eventually be born. Through everything, God was working out His plan to restore to humanity what had been lost and to create a people of His own.

Study Questions

Before you begin your study this week:

- ૐ Pray and ask God to speak to you through His Holy Spirit.
- ૐ Use only the Bible for your answers.
- ૐ Write down your answers and the verses you used.
- ૐ Answer the "Challenge" questions if you have the time and want to do them.
- ૐ Share your answers to the "Personal" questions with the class only if you want to share them.

First Day: Read the Commentary on Genesis 12-50.

1. What meaningful or new thought did you find in the Commentary on Genesis 12-50, or from your teacher's lecture? What personal application did you choose to apply to your life?

2. Look for a verse in the lesson to memorize this week. Write it down, carry it with you, tack it to your bulletin board, on the dashboard of your car, etc. Make a real effort to learn the verse and its "address" (reference of where it is found in the Bible).

3. This week's questions focus on the book of Exodus. If you have time, you may want to read through the entire book this week. As you answer the questions, you will be looking up passages of Scripture from various places in the Bible. This will help you discover that God's Word is a "whole," and that His message to us is the same from Genesis to Revelation.

Exodus shows us God's answer to our need. It is a picture of redemption—of God's activity to redeem us from our sin, degradation and misery. It illustrates for us what God has done and is doing in our lives.

Second Day:

Exodus 1-5 contains the complete story that we will cover in today's questions. If you can, you may want to read it in its entirety.

1. a. About three and one half centuries passed between the end of Genesis and the opening of Exodus. Jacob's (Israel's) family of 70—that had journeyed to Egypt to escape the famine—multiplied, and the land was filled with them. Read Exodus 1:10-11. What was the attitude of the Egyptians toward the Israelites, and why did they feel this way?

   b. Read Exodus 1:12-21. How did the Egyptian king attempt to weaken the Israelites? Whom did God use to thwart the king's plans, and how did He bless them for this? (Summarize briefly.)

2. a. Read Exodus 2:1-10. Summarize the circumstances of Moses' birth and how God preserved his life.

   b. Read Hebrews 11:23. How were Moses' parents able to hide him from the king?

3. a. Read Acts 7:22-28, which gives additional information about Moses. What was Moses like while he was in Egypt? (Acts 7:22)

   b. Did Moses know he was an Israelite? (Acts 7:23,25)

   c. What situation arose, how did Moses handle it, and why? (Acts 7:23-25)

   d. What was the response of one of the Israelites to Moses and his actions? (Acts 7:26-28)

4. a. Read Exodus 2:15. How did Pharaoh[1] react when he heard what Moses had done?

    b. What was Moses' response when he realized that his action had been discovered?

5. Read Exodus 2:21 and 3:1a, and Acts 7:29-30. What do you learn about Moses' life while he was in Midian? How long did he reside there?

6. a. What additional information about Moses do you learn from Hebrews 11:24-27? How was he able to do these things?

    b. Personal: After reading about Moses from several books of the Bible, we see that although his judgment was not always correct, he had faith. He even persevered for forty years in Midian by faith. Perhaps you are discouraged because you've prayed and not yet seen an answer to your prayer, or perhaps you believe God has called you to do something specific, but the doors have not yet opened for you to accomplish what He has called you to do. Read Hebrews 10:35-36 and personalize it by inserting your name into the passage. How do this passage and today's lesson encourage you?

Third Day:

1. Read Exodus 2:23-25. What happened during the time that Moses was in Midian?

2. a. Read Acts 7:30-32a. How did God get Moses' attention?

    b. How did God refer to Himself?

3. a. Read Acts 7:32b-33. How did Moses respond to the Lord?

    b. Why was Moses commanded to remove his shoes?

    c. Personal: Many people forget that God is holy. Some take a casual approach to God, as if He were the "good buddy upstairs." What is your attitude toward God? How can you show Him the honor and respect that is due Him?

4. Read Acts 7:34. God was aware of what was going on with His people, the Israelites. What did He plan to do about their situation?

5. God is aware of the situations in your life, too. Read Psalm 139:1-3 and describe how aware He is of your life.

6. Personal: Do you sometimes forget that God is concerned about everything in your life? Personalize 1 Peter 5:7 by changing "your" to "my," and "you" to "me."

Fourth Day:

1. a. In preparing to deliver the Israelites from bondage in Egypt, God sent Moses to Israel's leaders (see Exodus 3:13-18). Read Exodus 4:1-9. What was Moses' concern? (Exodus 4:1)

---

1. Pharaoh was the Egyptian king's title.

   b. What signs did God give to Moses? (Exodus 4:2-4, 6-7, 9)

   c. Why did God give these signs? (Exodus 4:5,8)

2. a. Read Exodus 4:10-17. What was Moses' excuse for not wanting to go, and how did God address this? Was God angry with Moses for these initial doubts? (Exodus 4:10-12)

   b. What did Moses say that finally angered the Lord? How did God eliminate Moses' final excuse for not going? (Exodus 4:13-17)

   c. Challenge: Why do you think God was angry? Hebrews 11:6a may give you additional food for thought.

3. a. Taking the rod of God with him, Moses, along with his brother Aaron, went to Egypt, where he immediately came into conflict with Pharaoh. God moved in mighty power against Pharaoh, who time and time again refused to let the Israelites go. (You can read about this in depth in Exodus 6-12). Read Exodus 12:21-22. What were the Israelites instructed to do?

   b. Read Exodus 12:12-13,23. Why were they to do this?

   c. Read Exodus 12:29-30. Did God's judgment come?

4. God allows sin and wickedness to continue for just so long, and then, as has happened throughout the ages,[1] His judgment comes. What do the following verses say regarding God's judgment?

Acts 17:31

Romans 2:5-6

5. God's judgment is certain, but 1 Corinthians 5:7b tells us that Christ, our Passover lamb, has been sacrificed for us. The Israelites, who by faith took the blood of a lamb and sprinkled it on the top and both sides of their door posts, were safe from God's judgment. What does Romans 5:8-9 tell us about Jesus Christ, who is our Passover lamb?

6. Personal: What new truth have you learned from today's study questions? What difference does this truth make to you personally?

Fifth Day:

1. Read Exodus 12:31-36. How did Pharaoh and the Egyptians react to God's final judgment on them, the death of their firstborn?

---

1. As in the Flood in Noah's day; the destruction of Sodom and Gomorrah; and the destruction of the Canaanites.

2. a. Read Exodus 12:37. The Israelites had been seventy in number when they entered Egypt. How many were they when they left Egypt?

    b. Read Exodus 12:40-41. How long had the Israelites been in Egypt?

3. God went before the Israelites in a pillar of cloud by day and a pillar of cloud by night. God did not lead the Israelites by the quickest route to the land He had promised them. From Exodus 13:17, what was the reason?

4. When Pharaoh again changed his mind and sent his army after the Israelites, who were camped next to the Red Sea, God again showed His power on behalf of Israel. Read Nehemiah 9:11 with Exodus 14:31. What happened?

5. Personal: The Israelites' passage through the Red Sea typifies our break with the world. There are people who are willing to sit under the Passover blood, who are willing to receive Jesus Christ as Savior, but they are not willing to walk through the way that God has opened for them. They never take that step which burns their bridges and cuts them off from the world, and their lives remain barren and unfruitful. Have you made that choice? Do you truly want all that God has for you, even though it means turning your back on the things of this world? Take a few minutes right now to think about this and talk to God about your attitude—whatever it may be.

Sixth Day:

1. Read Exodus 15:1a. How did the Israelites respond to their deliverance?

2. a. Read Nehemiah 9:12-20. Summarize what God did for the Israelites (verses 12-15), and what their response was (verses 16-17a, 18).

    b. Why didn't God destroy them? (Nehemiah 9:17b, 19-20)

3. a. It was on Mount Sinai that God gave the law, which is the revelation of His holy character. He also gave the tabernacle, which was His provision for dwelling with Israel, and He gave an intricate system of sacrifices and rituals for bringing the people into His presence—represented by the Most Holy Place within the tabernacle. Read Hebrews 10:1-4. Why were these things not the final answer to humanity's problem of sin?

    b. Read Hebrews 10:10-14. How is it possible for a holy, unchangeable God to dwell with us?

4. The law reveals God's holy, unchanging character. From Romans 7:7 and Galatians 3:24-25, what else does the law do for us?

5. Personal: Exodus gives us a concise picture of God's holiness, faithfulness, and mercy. It shows us the lengths He has gone to so that He might dwell among us. Let us thank Him for all that He accomplished on our behalf through the sacrifice of Jesus Christ. Write a prayer or psalm of thanksgiving to the Lord.

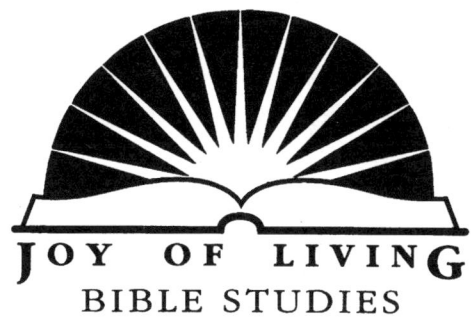

JOY OF LIVING
BIBLE STUDIES

HIGHLIGHTS OF THE OLD TESTAMENT
PART 1: HISTORY (GENESIS - ESTHER)
Lesson 4

Exodus: God's Answer to Humanity's Need[1]

Exodus, the second book of the Bible, is derived from the Greek word *exodos*, and means "exit" or "departure." As with the other four books in the Pentateuch (the Greek name for the first five books of the Hebrew Bible), God led Moses to write Exodus. The Scriptures themselves teach that Moses recorded what God revealed to him. In Nehemiah 9:14 we read, "You...gave them commands, decrees and laws through your servant Moses." Numbers 33:2 says, "At the Lord's command Moses recorded the stages in their journey."

The book of Genesis revealed to us the need of humanity for forgiveness of sin and a relationship with their Creator—and hinted at God's remedy. Now Exodus reveals God's answer to human need—His remedy for our sin and the restoration of fellowship with Him. In Genesis we saw God's plan of redemption begin to unfold in His promise to make of Abraham a great nation through whom all the peoples of the earth would be blessed, for through them would come the Savior of the world. In Exodus we will see the development of that nation.

Although we cannot be certain of the dates of the events of Exodus, it is generally accepted that the beginning of the oppression of the Israelites was about 1550 B.C. The story of Exodus begins in ancient Egypt, whose history and culture are well documented.

The narrative commences with God's activity in the preservation and call of Moses, whom God would eventually use in the transformation of a multitude of slaves into the nation of Israel. But that is not the whole story of Exodus. Within its pages is revealed forgiveness of sin by the shedding of blood, which points us to the Savior, "the Lamb of God, who takes away the sin of the world" (John 1:29).

Exodus centers around four great events: the Passover, the crossing of the Red Sea, the giving of the law at Sinai, and the construction of the tabernacle and its accompanying regulations for Israel. The first two events are but two aspects of one great truth—the deliverance of God's people from the bondage of Egypt. They also portray in Christian experience one great truth, which we call *conversion* or *regeneration*—the deliverance of an individual from the bondage of the world. The other two events likewise tie together. The pattern of the tabernacle was given by God to Moses at the same time that the law was given. The law requires the tabernacle, and the tabernacle exists because of the law.

1. This is an overview. You can study Exodus in more detail in the Joy of Living study, *Exodus: From Egypt to the Promised Land*.

Observing the Passover (Exodus 1-13)

When a person wants to change history he or she usually uses a battle or a ballot, but when God wants to change history He begins by sending a baby. Exodus opens some 300 years after the close of Genesis. The opening chapter informs us that a new king had arisen over Egypt who did not know Joseph. The original 70 Israelites had multiplied to an estimated two million. The new pharaoh greatly feared the power of this developing nation within Egypt, and gave orders that all male Hebrew children should be killed at birth.

Against this dark background, Moses was born. The story of his first 80 years is given to us in one brief chapter. In a delicate twist of irony, God moved in such a way that despite Pharaoh's decree, Moses was not only saved, but Pharaoh's daughter also adopted him and hired Moses' own mother to care for him. Moses was reared in the court of Pharaoh and had access to all the learning of the Egyptians. As the son of Pharaoh's daughter, he had every privilege.

When Moses came of age, he realized that he was destined to be the one who would deliver Israel from the bondage of the Egyptians. He attempted this in his own way, and ended up murdering a man and having to flee Egypt to escape the wrath of Pharaoh. He spent the next 40 years in the desert of Midian herding sheep for the man who became his father-in-law. All this was part of God's training. What Moses could not learn in Egypt, he must learn in the desert. The exalted prince became a humble shepherd. In Egypt he had learned human wisdom; in the desert he was to learn dependence on God.

It was here that God appeared to Moses in the burning bush. Moses' response to God's call was to doubt himself. "Who am I?" he cried out (Exodus 3:11). To this God replied, "I will be with you." Again Moses doubted, based on his ignorance of God. "Who are You?" is the essence of his query. The answer was, "I AM WHO I AM." In its full intent, this is the name of the Lord "who is, and who was, and who is to come, the Almighty" (Revelation 1:8). Yet again Moses doubted, and this time his doubt is of the people of Israel. "What if they do not believe me or listen to me and say, 'The LORD did not appear to you'?" (Exodus 4:1). God understood this fear, and granted him three signs: the staff, which could become a snake; the hand, which could become leprous and restored; and water, which could become blood. Yet again Moses doubted his qualifications; the eloquent prince of Egypt (see Acts 7:22) had become the inarticulate shepherd of Midian. God dismissed Moses' argument by reminding him who He was and what He could do.

All Moses' fears had been met by the revelation of the grace and power of God, but still Moses was reluctant to go, and he asked that someone else be sent in his place. At this the Lord became angry—He wanted faith and obedience, not ability. God answered Moses' reluctance by giving him Aaron, his brother, as a spokesman. Together, Moses and Aaron repeatedly confronted the obdurate and stubborn Pharaoh, and God's mighty power was revealed through a series of plagues, with which He revealed His supremacy over the satanic power personified in Pharaoh.

Chapter 11 describes the conversation between God and Moses in which the final plague, the final judgment on all the gods of Egypt that would cause Pharaoh to let the Israelites go, was predicted. When this happened, Israel was to ask the Egyptians for gold and silver, so that they might leave Egypt with an abundance.

This brings us to the feast of the Passover, which is a picture of God's redemptive plan for humanity. The Lord gave detailed instructions on how the Passover lamb should be killed and the blood placed on the door-frames of the houses, followed by the eating of the unleavened bread.

At midnight the Lord would go throughout Egypt and strike down all the firstborn in the land of Egypt, from that of Pharaoh to that of the slave girl, even the firstborn of the livestock. But when the Lord would see the blood of the lamb on the door-frames of the Israelites, He would pass over them—no plague would touch them. On that very night the Egyptians urged the Israelites to leave, thrusting their gold and silver upon them. Six hundred thousand men, besides women and children, left, and many who were not Israelites also went with them.

Every Israelite was commanded to teach the meaning of this Passover to his children. Centuries later, when John the Baptist would meet Jesus of Nazareth at the Jordan River, his announcement, "Look, the Lamb of God, who takes away the sin of the world!" (John 1:29), would be understood by every Israelite present. The Passover feast pictures for us the sacrifice of Christ on the cross, where the judgment of God was vented against all that is sinful within us, and only those who by faith rest under the protecting blood of the Lamb are saved.

Crossing the Red Sea (Exodus 14)

As the Israelites began their journey, God went before them in a pillar of cloud by day and a pillar of fire by night, to guide them on the way. The people went out into the desert, led by God, to the shores of the Red Sea. Looking back, they saw 600 Egyptian chariots hot upon their trail; looking ahead, they saw only the waters of the Red Sea. They were terrified and cried out to the Lord, and asked Moses why he had brought them there to die in the desert.

Moses said, "Do not be afraid. Stand firm and you will see the deliverance the LORD will bring you today" (Exodus 14:13). God's word came immediately to Moses, "Raise your staff and stretch out your hand over the sea to divide the water so that the Israelites can go through the sea on dry ground" (Exodus 14:16). The pillar of cloud moved between Israel and the Egyptians, creating darkness for the Egyptians and giving light to the Israelites. Throughout the night a great east wind drove back the waters of the sea and the people marched through the sea on dry ground, the waters standing as a wall on either side. When the Egyptians attempted to pursue them, the waters flowed back upon them, and they all died.

The Red Sea typifies a break with the world. Once Israel passed through the Red Sea, they were still in the desert, but they were out of Egypt. The sea now rolled between them and the place of bondage, and that same sea rolls between the Christian and the world when he claims Jesus Christ as Lord. Here is perhaps the reason why many professions of Christian faith never seem to go anywhere. There are people who are willing to sit under the Passover blood, willing to receive Jesus Christ as Savior, but they are not willing to walk through the parted waters of the Red Sea. They never take that step which brings them to the other side and cuts them off from the world. In their mind and thinking they are still back in Egypt. They will not move forward through the sea, and until that happens they are still under the bondage and control of the world.

Bitterness and Rest (Exodus 15)

We have in chapter 15 the story of the bitter waters of Marah. After three days without water, the people grumbled against Moses, who cried out to the Lord. To cure the waters of their bitterness, the Lord showed Moses a piece of wood. When Moses threw it into the water, the water became sweet. This is a symbol to us that the cross, that great piece of wood on which the Lord Jesus hung, is God's answer to the bitterness of life. When we have experienced the safety of the Passover and passed through the Red Sea, cutting ourselves off from the world, we discover that the cross is forever the answer to the bitterness that sin may have brought into our lives, both past and present.

After this the Lord brought them to Elim, a place of twelve springs and seventy palm trees. There they camped and rested. Marah as well as Elim were in the path on which God was leading them. In our lives, God's guidance may lead us through difficult places, but if we allow Him, He will take that which is bitter and turn it into that which is sweet. Then, in His time, He will bring us to a place of rest.

Grumbling and Grace (Exodus 16-18)

In chapters 16-18 we have the account of Israel's first experiences in the desert. They provide a continuing contrast between the grumbling, unbelieving people and the patient mercy of God. In response to His people's need for sustenance, God's first supernatural provision was the gift of manna, the bread from heaven. Israel was given clear instructions: for five days they were to gather just enough each day for that day, and on the sixth day they were to to gather enough for that day and the following day, the Sabbath. The people had difficulty in obeying, even as today. We also find it difficult to trust God for His provision in the midst of impossible situations.

Again their faith was tried when they came to a barren desert, where there was no water at all, but again God patiently met their grumbling unbelief by miraculously providing water out of the rock for them. They encountered a third trial when they suddenly found themselves under attack from the Amalekites. Joshua led the men in actual fighting while Moses, assisted by Aaron and Hur, prayed on the mountainside. The Israelites, through this experience, learned that faith requires obedient action, combined with dependence on God.

Giving of the Law (Exodus 19-24)

God called Moses and announced to him that if Israel would obey Him and keep His covenant, they, out of all the nations, would be to Him "a kingdom of priests and a holy nation" (Exodus 19:6). When Moses repeated these words to the people, their easy and superficial response was, "We will do everything the LORD has said" (Exodus 19:8). They had no true consciousness of what these words meant.

God, therefore, directed Moses to separate the people from the mountain. For three days they were to consecrate themselves, after which the Lord would come down on the mountain in the sight of all the people. On the third day there was thunder and lightning, a thick cloud upon the mountain, and a piercing trumpet blast, which made the whole camp of Israel tremble. Moses and Aaron were summoned to the mountain, and Moses alone was called into the very presence of God. There the voice of God delivered to him the words which we call the Ten Commandments.

The first five commandments dealt with the relationship between God and people, and especially guarded against the violation of God's person. The first warned against polytheism, and the second against idolatry. The third proclaimed the righteousness of God and warned against profanity. The fourth guarded the worship of God against secularism, and the fifth required the honoring of father and mother as representatives of God, guarding against irreverence to authority. The second five commandments concerned relationships between persons—guarding the sanctity of life, the sanctity of marriage, the sanctity of property, the sanctity of character, and the sanctity of the inner thought-life.

Instructions were also given as to the nature of worship, and it is significant that the only altar which God will honor was to be made of simple, unadorned stones, devoid of any human workmanship in which the human heart might boast. Thus the people were instructed in two essential matters: the law, which describes the character and holiness of God, and the system of sacrifice, by which a sinful and lawbreaking people might yet draw near to a holy and righteous God, and find Him merciful and gracious toward them.

Chapters 21-23 give ordinances which apply the principles of the ten commandments to life. The first section dealt with the rights of persons, wrong done to other people, and injuries brought about through neglect or carelessness. The second section dealt with the rights of property, covering theft and dishonesty. The third section touched upon matters which directly affected worship, including seduction, sorcery, bestiality and idolatry. Great concern was shown for the rights of strangers, indicating that God hears the cry and avenges the sorrows of many who are oppressed. Warnings were given against reviling

God and cursing rulers, and the rights of God concerning the firstborn were reiterated. Finally, matters of justice were detailed, and the three great feasts which Israel was to keep each year were described—the Feast of Unleavened Bread, associated with the Passover; the Feast of Weeks, later associated with Pentecost; and the Feast of Harvest at the end of the year.

These divine admonitions conveyed by Moses to the people concluded with God's great promise to send His angel before them to guard them and to bring them to the place that God had prepared. This angel is surely to be identified with Him who eventually became flesh and dwelt among us. He would ensure God's blessing to the people and drive out all their enemies.

Following these ordinances, Moses and Aaron and 70 of the elders of Israel were called upon, and Moses in their presence repeated all the words of the Lord, reading them as they were written in the Book of the Covenant. Taking blood from the altar, he sprinkled the people as they responded, "We will do everything the LORD has said; we will obey" (Exodus 24:7).

At this solemn point, the elders of Israel were invited to ascend the mountain further, where they saw the glory of God. Following this, Moses alone was called to the top of the mountain, where he waited for six days. On the seventh day he disappeared into the cloud of glory, which, in sight of the people of Israel, was like a consuming fire on the top of the mountain. There he remained for 40 days and 40 nights, receiving direction and instruction from the Lord.

Constructing the Tabernacle (Exodus 25-31)

The directions given to Moses for the construction of the tabernacle, the dwelling place of God among the people, began with the three articles of furniture which were to be at the heart of the worship of Israel. First was the Ark of the Covenant, with its cherubim overshadowing the atonement cover, symbolizing the dwelling place of God. Second was the table for the bread of the Presence, a symbol of fellowship, reminding the people of their constant need for communion with God. The golden lampstand followed, symbolizing the revelation these people were to receive and the testimony they were subsequently to give to the outside world.

Next, the divine details of the curtains and coverings of the tabernacle were specified. The curtain which separated the Holy Place from the Most Holy Place is interpreted in Hebrews 10:19-20 as the flesh of our Lord. When Jesus died, the curtain of the temple was torn in two, and a new and living way was opened up into the presence of God by Jesus' death. Exodus 27 describes the courtyard surrounding the tabernacle, beginning with the bronze altar on which the animal sacrifices were to be burned, which was to be set in front of the entrance to the Holy Place. Oil was commanded to be brought for the continuing light of the lampstand. This symbolized the Holy Spirit, who gives the light of revelation in the midst of the darkness of human knowledge.

Moses was next given instructions concerning the priesthood, which was to be vested in Aaron and his sons from the tribe of Levi.

Aaron, as high priest, foreshadowed the work of Christ, as confirmed by the book of Hebrews. The garments of the high priest, with their colors of gold, purple, scarlet and white, were to represent the glory, beauty, and work of Christ as our High Priest.

The consecration of the priests to their office is described in chapter 29. The washing symbolized the forgiveness of sin, the dressing signified imputation of righteousness, and the anointing spoke of the imbuing of the Holy Spirit. The offerings which follow emphasize anew the truth that the Lord wants always to be in the minds of His people—involved in every aspect of their lives, and that He could meet with them only through sacrifice and the cleansing of sin. By these means and these alone would a living God be able to dwell among a sinful people.

At this point the altar of incense is introduced. It completes the furniture of the Holy Place, and speaks of the offering of praise and adoration unto God. The bronze basin, which stood before the entrance of the Holy Place within the courtyard and symbolizes the necessity of cleansing from sin prior to entrance into God's presence, is then described. Finally, instruction is given concerning the use of anointing oil and incense.

The Lord who gave these instructions also called and equipped workmen to construct the tabernacle and all its furnishings. Two men, Bezalel of Judah and Oholiab of Dan, were filled with the Spirit of God and given the skill, ability and knowledge to perform this work. Then God commanded all the people to observe the Sabbath, signifying that the energy by which they labored was to be that of those who have entered into God's rest and have ceased from their own labors.

While these careful instructions were being given to Moses on the mountaintop, the people at the bottom of the mountain were already falling into grievous sin. The people who had so wondrously been redeemed from Egypt, led through the waters of the Red Sea, fed miraculously by manna from heaven, and refreshed by water from the rock, were now making and worshiping a golden calf. In a scene reminiscent of Abraham pleading with God for the salvation of Sodom and Gomorrah, we see Moses pleading before God on behalf of this people. As with Abraham, it was God Himself who was using Moses to call upon His mercy and allay His wrath. Moses pleaded not so much for the people, but for God Himself. He reminded Him that His honor was at stake, and pleaded the covenant made with Abraham, Isaac and Jacob. He thus became the instrument to turn aside the divine wrath.

On coming down from the mountain with the tablets of stone and surveying the scene of idolatry and debauchery, Moses angrily threw the tablets to the ground, breaking them. He ground the golden calf to powder and compelled the people to drink of the water into which it was thrown. He called, "Whoever is for the LORD, come to me" (Exodus 32:26). In response, the Levites gathered to him; he sent them throughout the camp with a sword in every hand, and 3,000 of the worst offenders were killed. The next day he returned to the presence of God, and there confessed the sin of the people and pleaded that they might be spared, even if he himself must be blotted out of God's book. God responded by sending him back again to lead the people

and promising the angel of His presence to go with him. Though the angel would go before the people to Canaan, God indicated that He would not dwell among them in their sinful state. This remoteness is indicated by the Tent of Meeting being placed outside the camp, where God would commune with Moses.

Chapters 35 to 39 contain the account of the actual construction of the tabernacle. When the work was finished, the cloud covered the Tent of Meeting and the glory of the Lord came down and filled the whole of the tabernacle. So splendid was this glory that Moses was not able to enter the tabernacle. Moreover the cloud of glory remained over the tabernacle as a permanent guide. Throughout the years of their wanderings it was to be a symbol to the people of the presence of God and the sign of God's instruction to move or to settle.

What will we make of this amazing building and its precise God-given design? In Hebrews 3:5-6 we are told, "Moses was faithful as a servant in all God's house, testifying to what would be said in the future. But Christ is faithful as a son over God's house. And *we are his house*, if we hold on to our courage and the hope of which we boast" (italics added). There the full meaning of the tabernacle is stated plainly—it was the symbol of Christ because Christ was the perfect man, but it was also the symbol of every believer in Christ who is indwelt by the Lord.

As the tabernacle in the desert was built in three parts—the courtyard, the Holy Place, and the Most Holy Place—so each person is a threefold construction consisting of body, soul and spirit. The human spirit is intended to be the dwelling place of the Holy Spirit, and this is symbolized by the Ark of the Covenant. The human soul corresponds to the Holy Place and its furniture. The table of the bread of the Presence, the golden lampstand, and the altar of incense reflect the qualities of *emotion* (expressing personality, which leads to fellowship), *mind* (encompassing knowledge which gives light), and *will* (making obedient choices which redound to the praise and glory of God). The courtyard symbolized the human body, with its exposure to the outside world. As Paul tells us in Romans 6, the body is the seat of sin, and therefore the site of the altar of sacrifice. It is also the place of defilement, and requires the cleansing work of the basin. But above all else, a person is to be the dwelling place of God, and the anointing of the Holy Spirit is to suffuse his being with the presence and power of God.

It is important to realize that if you are a Christian, the Lord Himself is dwelling in your body, which is His temple. Deep at the center of your life is the Most Holy Place, your human spirit, and in that place the Spirit of God dwells.

The great message of the book of Exodus is that God has made it possible for a holy, righteous God to dwell with sinful humans. Through symbols and pictures it foreshadowed what Jesus Christ would do on the cross for us. We must remember the great truth that God has so totally handled the problem of sin in the sacrifice of His Son that, as Paul says in Romans 8:1, "Therefore, there is now no condemnation for those who are in Christ Jesus." We have perfect access to the Father through the Son, and God's indwelling Spirit will never leave us or forsake us. He has taken up His abode in our hearts.

Study Questions

Before you begin your study this week:

- ৯ Pray and ask God to speak to you through His Holy Spirit.
- ৯ Use only the Bible for your answers.
- ৯ Write down your answers and the verses you used.
- ৯ Answer the "Challenge" questions if you have the time and want to do them.
- ৯ Share your answers to the "Personal" questions with the class only if you want to share them.

First Day: Read the Commentary on Exodus.

1. What meaningful or new thought did you find in the Commentary on Exodus, or from your teacher's lecture? What personal application did you choose to apply to your life?

2. Look for a verse in the lesson to memorize this week. Write it down, carry it with you, tack it to your bulletin board, on the dashboard of your car, etc. Make a real effort to learn the verse and its "address" (reference of where it is found in the Bible).

3. This week's questions focus on Leviticus. If you have time, you may want to read through the entire book this week. As you answer the questions, you will be looking up passages of Scripture from various places in the Bible. This will help you discover that God's Word is a "whole," and that His message to us is the same from Genesis to Revelation.

When people read through the Bible beginning at Genesis, Leviticus is probably where many stop reading. It is filled with ceremonies, sacrifices, dietary laws, and what seem to be meaningless restrictions. However, Leviticus is full of meaning—it is God's picture book to help us understand how an unholy people can approach a holy God. As we will see, each picture points to Jesus Christ.

Second Day:

1. a. In Leviticus 20:26a, what requirement did God place on the Israelites, and why?

   b. Read 1 Peter 1:15-16. What are we Christians called to be and why?

2. a. God demands holiness, but according to Romans 3:23 what problem does each and every person have?

   b. From the following verses, what problems does this present?

   Isaiah 59:2

   Habbakuk 1:13a

   Romans 6:23

   Colossians 1:21

3. a. We can see the seriousness of sin, and the impossibility of having fellowship with a holy God until our sin is dealt with. What does Hebrews 9:22 say regarding the forgiveness of sin?

   b. From Leviticus 1:4 and 17:11, how was this accomplished under the Law of Moses?

4. a. From Hebrews 10:1-4, what do you learn about the laws and sacrifices we will be studying in Leviticus?

    b. What does 1 John 1:7b say regarding what the blood of Jesus Christ can do?

5. As we said previously, the sacrifices of the Old Testament showed the seriousness of sin and pointed us to Jesus Christ. From Hebrews 10:10-12, compare the sacrifice of Jesus Christ and the sacrifices the priests made.

6. Personal: We are all sinful, unholy people separated from God, but thankfully we can be cleansed from our sin, made holy, and brought into a relationship with God because of the sacrifice of Jesus Christ. Have you put your faith in Jesus Christ? If not, you can pray right where you are. If you have, write briefly about when you first trusted Jesus Christ.

Third Day:

The offerings in Leviticus were pictures of what Jesus Christ would do for us, and they show what our attitude should be toward God.

1. a. The *burnt offering* is described in Leviticus 1. It pictures for us Jesus, the perfect sacrifice, who offered Himself completely for us. How do Romans 3:25a and 1 Peter 1:18-19 express this?

    b. As Jesus offered Himself completely, we too are to offer ourselves completely to the Lord. What does Matthew 22:37 say regarding this?

2. a. The *grain offering* is described in Leviticus 2. It was a daily offering, and represents life. How do John 6:48,51 and Colossians 3:4a express that Jesus Christ provides life?

    b. Just as the grain offering symbolized life and was offered daily, what do Romans 12:1 and Colossians 3:17 say regarding our own lives?

3. a. The *fellowship offering* is described in Leviticus 3. Fellowship implies a relationship. From 2 Corinthians 5:18a, how are we brought into relationship with God?

    b. Once we have fellowship with God, we have access to the peace of God. What does Philippians 4:6-7 say regarding the peace of God, and how do Christians obtain it?

4. a. The *sin offering* is described in Leviticus 4:1—5:13. It addresses both public and private sin, as well as both known and unknown sin. Read Leviticus 4:27-28. Is a person still guilty before God if they didn't intend to sin? What must they do when they are made aware of their sin?

    b. From Romans 5:8 and 8:3, describe the Christian's sin offering.

5. The *guilt offering* is described in Leviticus 5:14—6:7. While the sin offering dealt with the nature which causes us to sin, the guilt offering dealt with the actual acts of evil we commit, including acts of commission as well as those of omission. The unique characteristic of the guilt offering was that it required both sacrifice and restitution. It was necessary to right the wrong which had been done, as far as it could be corrected. How is this truth expressed in Matthew 5:23-24 and 1 John 4:10-11?

6. Personal: After looking at each of the sacrifices and their meaning, what do you want to change in your life? Why not pray about this now?

Fourth Day:

In Leviticus 8-10 we will see that the second element required for a proper walk and worship before God is that of the priesthood. Perhaps you noticed in yesterday's questions that only a priest could offer sacrifices. The priests were the "go-between" between God and the individual Israelite. All priests were of the tribe of Levi and descended from Aaron; the other Levites were their assistants. Leviticus 8-10 contains strict laws regarding a priest's sanctification, behavior, and duties.

1. Read Hebrews 10:12, which speaks of Jesus Christ. Why is it no longer necessary for us to have a priesthood and offer animal sacrifices?

2. a. Read Hebrews 4:14-16. From verse 14, who is our High Priest?

    b. From verse 15, describe our High Priest's holiness.

    c. From verse 16, since His sacrifice fulfills all of God's requirements, what may we now do?

3. Personal: Jesus Christ is the perfect man, the perfect sacrifice, and the perfect High Priest. Do you need forgiveness? Do you need help? Do you need grace? Whatever your need, go to Him—not in fear, but with confidence. He loves you and He understands.

Fifth Day:

Leviticus 11-22 deals with laws about food, health and daily living. Some are very practical precautions that doctors and scientists eventually discovered to be important, especially in ancient times. Others were symbolic of spiritual truths. All set forth the requirements for an unholy (unclean) people to have a relationship with our Holy God. All required strict obedience.

1. Summarize Leviticus 22:31-33, making note of what the Israelites were to do and why.

2. Read Leviticus 17:11-12. Why were the people forbidden to eat the blood of animals?

3. a. The high priest was permitted into the Most Holy Place only once a year on the Day of Atonement, after atoning for the sin of his household and himself. From Leviticus 16:15-16, what was he to do, and why?

    b. From Leviticus 16:20-22, what else was the high priest to do, and why?

4. Read Hebrews 9:11-14. List the differences between the priests' actions and what they accomplished on the Day of Atonement and Jesus Christ's actions and what He accomplished.

5. Personal: Reading through Leviticus helps us understand that God takes His holiness very seriously, and so should we. What specifically has been meaningful to you, and how will it change your daily actions and attitudes?

Sixth Day:

If you would like to, read Leviticus 23-25, which discusses Old Testament feasts and sacred days. These were not mere holidays, to be observed on the nearest Monday in order to provide for a long weekend. Each was a symbolic occasion designed to teach a truth which God wants to impart to His people.

1. The *Sabbath* (see Leviticus 23:1-3), which occurred every seventh day, was a day to worship and rest, reminding the Israelites of God's finished work of *creation*. Christians celebrate God's finished work of *redemption* on the day Christ rose from the dead, the first day of the week. What do John 19:30 and Hebrews 10:10 say regarding Christ's sacrifice?

2. a. The *Passover* and *Feast of Unleavened Bread* (see Leviticus 23:4-8) reminded the Israelites that the work of redemption rested on another. What does 1 Corinthians 5:7 say regarding our Passover sacrifice?

   b. The *Feast of Firstfruits* (see Leviticus 23:9-15) fell on the day after the Sabbath, or Sunday, and was a fitting anticipation of the resurrection of Christ. What does 1 Corinthians 15:20 say about this?

   c. The waving of the two loaves before the Lord at the *Feast of Weeks* (see Leviticus 23:15-22), pictured the church, in which Jew and Gentile would be joined into one body. What does Romans 10:12 say about this?

3. Next we have the *Feast of Trumpets* (see Leviticus 23:23-25), which prophetically anticipated the prediction that Jesus would return to gather His people. Read Matthew 24:30-31 and describe this event.

4. The *Day of Atonement* (see Leviticus 23:26-32) was characterized as a time of affliction of spirit and of mourning for sin. We should never take sin lightly. What does James 4:8-10 say to Christians who are walking in sin?

5. Next was the *Feast of Tabernacles* (see Leviticus 23:33-44). From Leviticus 23:42-43, of what was this feast to remind the Israelites? (A "booth" is a temporary shelter.)

6. The *Sabbatical Year* (see Leviticus 25:1-7) was observed every seventh year to allow the land rest for a year. Symbolically, it points to a recognition of dependence upon God's ability to bring fruitfulness in social life, in interpersonal relationships, and even in governmental matters. What does John 15:1,4-5 say regarding the fruitfulness of our lives?

7. The *Year of Jubilee* (see Leviticus 25:8-24) came every fiftieth year, as an intensification of the Sabbatical Year. Characteristic of the Year of Jubilee was the proclamation of liberty to all the inhabitants of the land. The mark of liberty is to regain a lost inheritance and to have broken relationships restored. What does 1 Peter 1:3-5 say regarding the inheritance of those who have put their faith in Jesus Christ?

8. Personal: As we have seen, Leviticus is a picture-book of the inflexibility of God's love and righteousness. It is an inevitable rule of life that if you reject light, then you must endure darkness; if you will not receive the positive, then you must experience the negative; if you will not go in, then you must stay out—until the time comes when you are ready to go in. If there is repentance and return, there is also the promise of recovery and restoration. There are no other choices. What will your choices be, not only regarding eternal salvation, but also in living your everyday life? Make a list of changes you hope to make, and then ask God to help you.

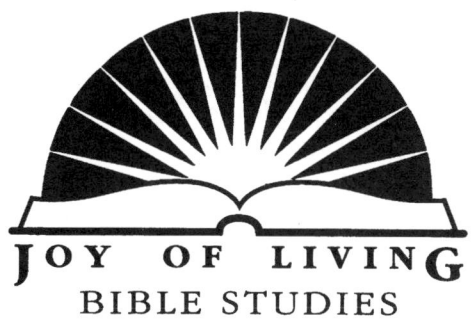

Leviticus: The Way to Wholeness

When people read through the Bible beginning at Genesis, Leviticus is probably where many stop reading. It is filled with ceremonies and sacrifices, problems of diet, and what may seem to be meaningless restrictions. If you want to understand Leviticus, one verse near the center of the book will help greatly, "You are to be holy to me because I, the LORD, am holy, and I have set you apart from the nations to be my own" (Leviticus 20:26). Leviticus is God's picture book to help us understand how an unholy people can approach a holy God and can enjoy a relationship so close that God will delight to say, "You are mine." As we will see, each picture points to Jesus Christ, who said, "I am the way and the truth and the life. No one comes to the Father except through me" (John 14:6).

Don't be put off by the word "holy" in this book. To many of us, "holy" people are those who look as if they had been steeped in vinegar. But the root from which the word *holy* is derived is the same root from which the word *wholeness* also comes. If you read "wholeness" in place of "holiness" everywhere you find it in the Bible, you will be much closer to what the writers originally meant. Wholeness is to have together all the parts which were intended to be there, and to have them function as they were intended to function. People were intended to function in relationship with God. All of our brokenness ultimately stems from our broken relationship with Him.

The men and women who lived before the time of the cross were as hurt and broken and fragmented as we are. They needed to be brought back into relationship with God. They, too, needed Christ, and through these sacrifices and rituals (which are pictures of Christ and what He would do), He was available to them. Any Israelite who, by faith, obediently and sincerely offered these sacrifices found that the reaction of the Spirit was to bring him to the same joy and peace that believers have today.

Leviticus falls into two basic divisions. The first part, chapters 1 through 16, reveals the fundamental needs of our humanity and God's provision for these needs. The second part, chapters 17 through 27, unfolds what performance God expects from us in response.

Humanity's Needs and God's Provision

Within the first half of Leviticus there are four elements traced which reveal the basic needs of sinful humanity.

The Need for Offerings (Leviticus 1-7)

The first element is a series of five offerings.

The Burnt Offering

For the burnt offering, the sacrifice was to be a male without blemish. The worshipper was to lay his hand on the head of the offering. That was God's way of teaching the great truth of substitution, the fact that we human beings are tied together with each other and belong to one another, and thus others can do things for us which we cannot do ourselves. In the case of dealing with sin, the substitute must be a spotless, sinless person. Thus, Jesus Christ is the only adequate substitute, and this was symbolized by the burnt offering.

The next step was to kill the sacrificial animal. God never allowed any compromise on this. He did not say, "This is a nice little lamb and is innocent of any wrongdoing himself, so if you'll just drain a half pint of blood from him, I'll be satisfied." God desires to impress upon us the fact that the problem He is dealing with is so intense and so deeply rooted in our human lives that nothing but death itself can solve it. The blood was sprinkled against the altar and the sacrifice was burned as an act of consecration and commitment to God. The animal was to be totally consumed by the fire on the altar. No one was ever to eat the meat of the burnt offering.

This burnt offering was the first of three sacrifices that were said to be "an aroma pleasing to the LORD." It symbolized the great truth that in order to fulfill the dominion over the earth given to humanity, we must ourselves be given wholly to God. The testimony of all history is that we are very unhappy until we are possessed by God.

The final distinction of the burnt offering was that the fire on the altar must never be allowed to go out. This symbolized the truth that our basic identity before God is the fact upon which all the rest of life must rest. If you stand there, you have a basis upon which all the other relationships of life can be worked out.

The Grain Offering

The grain offering consisted of flour, loaves of bread, or grains offered before the Lord. The essence of this offering was that it was bread, the staff of life. Since it was bloodless, it did not symbolize a death, but rather a life. In the New Testament Jesus said, "I am the bread of life...If anyone eats of this bread, he will live forever" (John 6:48,51). The gospel consists not only of the death of Jesus but also of His life made available to us. Jesus Christ died *for you* in order that He might live *in you.*

Oil, incense and salt were always included in the grain offering. The oil was both mingled with the flour and poured on top of it, picturing the indwelling Spirit who mingles with our humanity, and also the anointing of the Spirit which is to empower us. Incense was a delight to God, and spoke of praise and thanksgiving, which pleases Him. Salt, a preservative, spoke of a life which reaches out to touch others with good effect. It is our righteous influence. Yeast and honey were always excluded. Yeast was a picture of sin, because it has the power to puff up. By this God was saying, "When you come to offer your humanity to me, there must be no ego in it: do not do this for your own glory." Honey is natural sweetness. There are people who have a natural, even temper. They are naturally sweet. But God refused to accept this as an offering—the only sweetness He will accept is the imparted sweetness of Jesus Christ in you.

The burnt offering indicated God reaching out to humanity and saying, "You are mine." The grain offering pictured humanity's response. We must come to Him and say, "Lord, here I am; here is my redeemed humanity with its oil and its incense and its salt, but with no yeast and with no honey. I want to be yours; I give myself to you."

The Fellowship Offering

In the phrase "fellowship offering," the word translated "fellowship" includes the ideas of health, wholeness, welfare, and peace.[1] Fellowship based on peace *with* God, resulting in the peace *of* God, is what this sacrifice depicted—the sense of calmness, of serenity, of the untroubled heart which was so continually manifested in Jesus. It is of this He spoke when He said, "Peace I leave with you; my peace I give you" (John 14:27).

The Sin Offering

The sin offering pictured the way God deals with the alienation which prevents us from receiving His grace. This offering provided for both public and private sin. It was frequently offered when the individual had sinned unknowingly. Thus this offering dealt not so much with the act of evil, but with the nature which prompts such acts.

The Guilt Offering

While the sin offering dealt with the nature which causes us to sin, the guilt offering dealt with the actual acts of evil we commit, including both acts of commission and omission. The unique characteristic of the guilt offering was that it required both sacrifice and restitution. It was necessary to right the wrong which had been done, as far as it could be corrected.

Two classes of sins were covered by this offering. The first was that of religious offense, something done in regard to "the Lord's holy things" (Leviticus 5:15). Though the sin was an unintentional sin, the individual was required to offer a guilt offering and to make restitution. Thus even something done with utter conviction at the time that it was right, when discovered to be wrong, required sacrifice and restitution.

The other category of sin involved cheating, robbing, or defrauding a neighbor, or any other form of dishonesty, such as removing someone else's property or damaging their reputation. Such a broken relationship must be restored and restitution made. This is surely what Jesus refers to when He says: "Therefore, if you are offering your gift at the altar and there remember that your brother has something against you, leave your gift there in front of the altar. First go and be reconciled to your brother; then come and offer your gift" (Matthew 5:23-24). The guilt offering is given for the healing of all broken relationships and to give the offender a clear conscience before God and humanity.

The Need for a Priesthood (Leviticus 8-10)

The second element required for an adequate walk and worship before God is that of a priesthood. In the Old Testament the priesthood consisted of Aaron and his descendants. We find in these chapters the historical account of the consecration of the priests and the tabernacle, and the beginning of worship within the tabernacle. Aaron's first act as high priest was to bring a sin offering and burnt offering for himself, and then the offerings of the priests on behalf of the people are recorded. Moses (the prophet) and Aaron (the priest) came out of the tabernacle and blessed the people, and the glory of the Lord appeared to them all. The waiting throngs were stunned by the sudden appearance of fire from the Lord which consumed the offerings, and when the people saw it they shouted and fell on their faces.

Following this was the account of the two sons of Aaron, Nadab and Abihu, who offered unauthorized fire before the Lord. For this they were destroyed by a supernatural fire. The whole account helps us see that priesthood was a serious matter involving both privilege and responsibility.

We must always bear in mind, in reading these accounts, that there is no special priesthood today. All believers are made priests (see 1 Peter 2:5). Thus in the church, the Body of Christ, we are all to minister humbly to one another, bearing each other's burdens, rebuking and correcting one another, doing all with the knowledge that Jesus Christ is our Master and we all are brothers and sisters.

The Need for a Standard (Leviticus 11)

The third element of human need is a standard by which we may tell the difference between the true and the false, the phony and the real, the helpful and the hurtful. Various dietary laws and sanitary practices were given to preserve Israel from diseases rife in the nations around them. But not all the regulations were for health reasons. There was nothing wrong with many of the animals that were prohibited to Israel as food. They were prohibited only to teach a symbolic lesson. There were four spheres from which food could be taken.

First, there were the animals which walked about on the earth. Among these the Israelites were to eat only those which chewed the cud and also had a split hoof. This pictures for us the spiritual food upon which believers are to feed, the Word of God. First, we must meditate, which is pictured by the chewing of the cud. Second, we must distinguish between that which is from above and that which is from below, pictured by the dividing of the hoof. We must take note of the fact that the Bible reports the lies of Satan and the confused thinking of people, as well as the revelation of the mind of God.

Second, the Israelites were to take food from the sea, which is used throughout Scripture as a symbol of the world, of society. From

---

1. Frank E. Gaebelein, editor. *The Expositor's Bible Commentary* (Grand Rapids: Zondervan, 1990). See notes on Leviticus 3.

this area the proper food was to be distinguished by the possession of both fins and scales. Since fins are for progress and scales are for protection, this symbolizes our need to have both the capacity to penetrate a subject and yet to protect ourselves from any wrongful effect. We need both to understand and to discriminate, when feeding upon the knowledge of the world and its ways.

The third sphere from which food could come was the heavens. All birds that fed upon flesh were forbidden. Since the heavens are clearly the realm of the spirit, we are dealing here with spiritual knowledge, especially in the realm of religion. We are clearly warned to reject all that is related to the flesh, that which is carnal in nature, arising out of the principle of self-sufficiency.

Finally, whatever creature moved about on the ground, went on its belly, or had many feet, was to be rejected. This immediately suggests the story of the Fall in the Garden of Eden and the curse which came upon the serpent, in that he was to crawl on his belly for the rest of his life (see Genesis 3:14). I believe this sphere represents knowledge based on satanic philosophy. It is wholly of the earth, relating only to this present life—its standards, its values, its pride, and its glory. We are not to feed upon these or accept them as principles on which to live.

The Need for Atonement (Leviticus 16)

The Day of Atonement detailed the provision God made for dealing with all sin, whether known or unknown, in His people. It was the one day of the year when the high priest would enter the Most Holy Place, dressed not in his garments of beauty and glory but in simple white linen undergarments, which spoke of humility and weakness. There he offered incense for himself, the blood of a bull for his priestly household, and the blood of a goat as a sin offering for the people. Upon the head of a second living goat all the sins of the people were confessed and symbolically placed, and the goat was led away into the desert.

Human Performance

Leviticus 17-27 describes the performance which is possible on the basis of the provision God has made. God never mentions performance until He has fully revealed His provision. He does not speak about behavior until He has made clear the power by which we are to act.

Basis for Wholeness (Leviticus 17)

First, we must understand that blood is the basis for wholeness (holiness). Many are offended by the amount of blood involved in the Old Testament sacrifices, but by this means God was telling us that the basis for wholeness is a life given up, that we can never be whole on the basis of our natural life. We must have a new kind of life, and to have it we must give up the old. Often the problem of the Christian life is that we keep trying to hang on to the old way of life and refuse to accept the new.

Standards for Purity (Leviticus 18-22)

Second was a series of practical guidelines for acting in love amid all the relationships of life. Leviticus 18 gave standards for purity, first in the family, and especially with regard to sexual morals—incest, marriage of close relatives, adultery, homosexuality, and bestiality, along with the terrible practice of the Canaanites, child sacrifice. There followed a section of general ethical prescriptions to which God, as it were, signed His own name 14 times. This was intended not only to indicate authority, but also to suggest resource. The various regulations were summed up in the admonition of Leviticus 19:18, "Love your neighbor as yourself. I am the LORD."

To enforce the standards for purity, Leviticus gave certain prescribed punishment. The death penalty was required for child sacrifice, for consulting with spirits, for cursing parents, for adultery and homosexuality, and for intercourse with animals. We must understand that in Christ, though these penalties are mitigated and opportunity is given for repentance and forgiveness, nevertheless the deeds are as wrong today as they were in Old Testament times.

Enjoyment of God (Leviticus 23-25)

Third was the enjoyment of the presence and power of God Himself. Here we learn the meaning of worship in Israel, and the provision for the compassionate distribution of wealth through the institution of the Sabbatical Year and the Year of Jubilee. The feasts of Israel were not mere holidays, to be observed on the nearest Monday in order to provide for a long weekend. Each was a symbolic occasion designed to teach a truth which God wanted to impart to His people that is fundamental to human happiness.

Sabbath

The Sabbath indicated that rest is at the heart of everything God requires. The secret is to learn how to operate out of rest. It is activity, growing out of dependence upon the work of Another, with the realization that the responsibility to achieve lies with Him.

Passover

The first of the set feasts was the Passover. It was God's graphic way of teaching that His work of redemption must rest upon the death of another on our behalf.

Feast of Unleavened Bread

The Feast of Unleavened Bread followed immediately after the Passover. Its central feature was the exclusion of all yeast. This pictures the cleansing of life from sin which must follow redemption.

Feast of Firstfruits

Following the Feast of Unleavened Bread, the Feast of Firstfruits fell on the day after the Sabbath, a Sunday. It was an anticipation of the resurrection of Christ, "the firstfruits of those who have fallen asleep" (1 Corinthians 15:20).

Feast of Weeks

Fifty days after the Feast of Firstfruits was the Feast of Weeks. It was characterized by two loaves of bread baked with yeast, which were waved before the Lord. Thus it pictures the church, made of two bodies—Jew and Gentile. Both are sinners needing redemption, but joined together into one body, the church.

Feast of Trumpets

The Feast of Trumpets followed the long summer in which no feast was held. It anticipated the prediction of Jesus that He will return "with a loud trumpet" (Matthew 24:31) to gather His people.

Day of Atonement

This was followed by the Day of Atonement, a time of mourning and confession of sin, when "all the nation's sins, failures and weaknesses of the people were atoned for. The blood was shed and the sins of the people were covered so that God could take up His abode in the midst of His people in spite of their uncleanness."[1]

Feast of Tabernacles

The last feast was the Feast of Tabernacles. It memorialized the time when, after Israel's deliverance from Egypt, they lived in tents while they journeyed in the desert.

Sabbatical Year

This brings us to the Sabbatical Year. Every seventh year Israel was to let the land rest for a year. They were not to sow crops or even to prune vineyards. This pointed to a recognition of dependence upon God's ability to bring fruitfulness in life.

Year of Jubilee

With this was linked the Year of Jubilee, which came every fiftieth year. Liberty was to be proclaimed to all the inhabitants of the land. The mark of liberty was to regain a lost inheritance and to have broken relationships restored. There is no record that Israel ever actually experienced the Year of Jubilee. In all their history they never trusted God enough to try it out to see what He would do, and so they never saw God's full supply.

Obedience Leads to Blessing (Leviticus 26)

God promised blessings upon the people if they would walk in faithfulness before Him, utilizing the provisions for cleansing which He had instituted. The promises were for fruitfulness, full supply, security, increase, and fellowship with Him, with the result that they would "walk with heads held high" (Leviticus 26:13).

But God moved on to set forth the punishments which would follow failure to walk in His ways: disease, conflict, drought, wild beasts, invasion, break-up of family life, and finally, captivity. All of this now stands written in history, but the wonderful thing is that through it all God has a redemptive, constructive goal toward which He aims. If there is repentance and return, there is also the promise of recovery and restoration.

Leviticus is the story of the inflexibility of God's love and righteousness. It is an inevitable rule of life that if you reject light, then you must endure darkness; if you will not receive the positive, then you must experience the negative; if you will not go in, then you must stay out—until the time comes when you are ready to go in. There are no other choices.

Observation of Vows (Leviticus 27)

The final chapter of the book dealt with the matter of vows. Vows are voluntary obligations which are promised to God, usually on the ground of some blessing from Him. The point was that it was not necessary to make vows, but if they were made they must be fulfilled. If for any reason the one making a vow desired to be set free from it, he must pay its full value, plus something more, according to the appraisal of the priest. Doubtless God uses such vows to draw us out and to help us grow in the discipline of grace. It is significant that the book which calls us preeminently to worship closes with regulations on how to handle the voluntary commitments of our hearts.

---

1. *What the Bible Is All About Bible Handbook*, p68.

Study Questions

Before you begin your study this week:
- ❧ Pray and ask God to speak to you through His Holy Spirit.
- ❧ Use only the Bible for your answers.
- ❧ Write down your answers and the verses you used.
- ❧ Answer the "Challenge" questions if you have the time and want to do them.
- ❧ Share your answers to the "Personal" questions with the class only if you want to share them.

First Day: Read the Commentary on Leviticus.

1. What meaningful or new thought did you find in the Commentary on Leviticus, or from your teacher's lecture? What personal application did you choose to apply to your life?

2. Look for a verse in the lesson to memorize this week. Write it down, carry it with you, tack it to your bulletin board, on the dashboard of your car, etc. Make a real effort to learn the verse and its "address" (reference of where it is found in the Bible).

3. This week's questions focus on Numbers and Deuteronomy. If you have time, you may want to read through the entire passage this week. As you answer the questions, you will be looking up passages of Scripture from various places in the Bible. This will help you discover that God's Word is a "whole," and that His message to us is the same from Genesis to Revelation.

Numbers opens in the desert of Sinai, in the second year after the Israelites had left Egypt. Deuteronomy opens close to the edge of the Promised Land, 40 years later. In between is the sad record of Israel's failure to believe God.

Second Day:

1. a. Read Numbers 1:1-3, 44-50. As the book of Numbers opens, what did God command Moses to do? (verses 1-3)

   b. What was the final count? (verses 44-46)

   c. Who was excluded from the count and why? (verses 47-50)

2. From Numbers 2:1-2, what was to be in the center of the Israelite camp?

3. a. Read Numbers 9:15-16. On the day the tabernacle was set up, what covered it? Describe its appearance by day and by night.

   b. Read Numbers 14:14. What was the meaning of this sight?

4. From Numbers 9:17-22, describe how God led the Israelites.

5. Personal: So we see that God was to be the center of the life of Israel. Each person had an appointed place, and they were guided by the Lord daily. God is supposed to be at the center of our lives too. We each have an appointed place within the Body of Christ (see 1 Corinthians 12), and our lives are to be directed by the Lord. Is He the center of your life? Are you following His leading? Are you fulfilling your place in the Body of Christ (the Church)? What changes do you need to make?

Third Day:

Numbers 11-25 records the people's discontent with God's provision and care. Remember that these people had been slaves, in "hard labor" in Egypt.

1. From Nehemiah 9:9-11, review and summarize what God had already done for these Israelites.

2. a. Read Exodus 3:17. God was not just delivering them from Egypt. What else had He promised them?

    b. God doesn't just deliver us from the kingdom of darkness. He took us out, to bring us in—into His kingdom (see Colossians 1:13). Describe His kingdom from Romans 14:17.

3. a. Read Psalm 78:14-32, which summarizes some of Israel's journey as they traveled through the desert toward the Promised Land. List the miraculous ways God provided for them. (verses 14-16, 23-29)

    b. List Israel's response to God's provision. (verses 17-22, 30-32)

4. Personal: Are you trusting God to lead you, or are you complaining that your life and your circumstances aren't the way you think they should be? Personalize 1 Peter 1:3-7 by inserting your name. Ask God to make 1 Peter 1:6 a reality in your life.

Fourth Day:

1. a. As the Israelites neared the Promised Land of Canaan, what did God instruct them to do? (Numbers 13:1-2)

    b. What report did they bring back? (Numbers 13:25-33, summarize briefly)

2. a. Read Numbers 14:1-9. How did the Israelites respond to the negative report of the ten spies? (verses 1-4)

   b. What did Joshua and Caleb (two of the spies) say to encourage the people? (verses 7b-9)

3. Read Numbers 14:26-38. What judgment did God pronounce on the Israelites? Who was exempt? (Summarize briefly.)

4. a. Read Numbers 14:39-45. How did the Israelites respond to God's pronouncement? (verses 39-40)

   b. How did Moses rebuke and warn them? (verses 41-43)

   c. How did the Israelites respond to Moses' warning, and what was the result? (verses 44-45)

5. Personal: After Moses led the Israelites out of Egypt, they promised, "We will do everything the Lord has said" (Exodus 19:8). But now, when God said, "Go," the people said, "No." Then when He said, "Don't go," they said, "We will go." Read Psalm 95:10, Proverbs 3:5-7, and Proverbs 16:25; then take a few minutes to search your own heart. Do you frequently go the way you think is right instead of truly seeking God's way?

Fifth Day:

After the Israelites were defeated by the inhabitants of the hill country, they finally obeyed God's command and turned back to begin their long period of wandering in the desert.

1. a. Read Hebrews 3:7-10, and describe the Israelites during those forty years in the desert.

   b. Read Nehemiah 9:19-21, and describe how God showed His compassion to them during that forty-year period.

   c. Personal: Pause and consider. Even in the midst of judgment, God was compassionate. If you would like to, write down your thoughts about this.

2. a. Read Numbers 21:4-9. Finally Israel's forty year wandering was over, and the new generation of Israelites was preparing to enter the Promised Land. What do you find out about this new generation? (verses 4-5)

   b. What was God's judgment on them for growing impatient and speaking against Him? What was the remedy? (verses 6-9)

3. The sentence of death is passed upon each of us because of our sin (see Romans 3:23 and 6:23). Read John 3:14-16. What is God's remedy?

4. Personal: Have you acknowledged your sin and looked in faith to Jesus Christ and the blood He shed on the cross, asking Him to forgive your sin and give you eternal life? If not, don't wait; today, this moment, please pray and ask God to forgive your sin because of Jesus Christ. Write down your thoughts about this.

Sixth Day:

Deuteronomy contains three great sermons delivered by Moses to the Israelites shortly before his death. These Israelites were a new generation who either were not yet born or were children when their fathers had been given the Law from Mount Sinai. As they were about to enter the land of Canaan, it was essential that they understand their history, God's law, and His requirements.

1. a. Read Deuteronomy 9:1-6 and describe the current inhabitants of the Promised Land. (verses 1-2)

    b. Who would give the Israelites victory? (verse 3)

    c. Why was God driving out the inhabitants of the land and giving it to the Israelites? (verses 4-6)

2. What does Deuteronomy 28:1-3, 15-16 say regarding the results of obedience and disobedience to the Lord?

3. a. Moses was not to be the one to lead the Israelites into the Promised Land. Joshua was to take his place. Read Deuteronomy 31:6-8. What encouraging words did God give to Israel and to Joshua?

    b. What word of encouragement does the Lord give you in Hebrews 13:5b?

4. a. God had used Moses to lead the people out of Egypt and through the desert. Through him, they were given God's law. Just prior to Moses' death at age 120, God allowed him to see the Promised Land from Mount Nebo. Summarize what Moses said to the Israelites in Deuteronomy 32:46-47.

    b. What does Jesus say regarding His words in John 6:63?

5. Read Romans 1:5. What results from true faith?

6. Personal: Your life bears witness to what you truly believe, to where your faith lies. What does your life say about you?

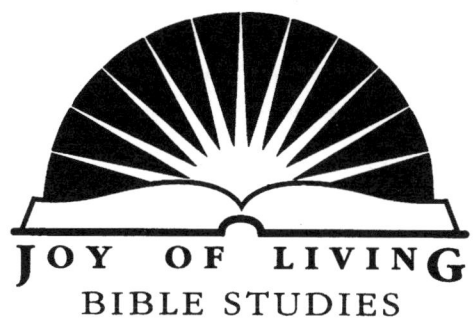

JOY OF LIVING
BIBLE STUDIES

Numbers & Deuteronomy—The Incomplete Life[1]

Numbers takes its title from the census with which it both begins and ends. It opens in the desert of Sinai, in the second year after Israel left Egypt, and closes at the edge of the Promised Land, 40 years later. In between is a long and sad record of the failure of Israel to believe in God's provision and power during their wanderings in the desert.

Numbers is a dramatic setting for what is perhaps the hardest lesson a Christian must learn—to trust God instead of their own reason. The book forms a commentary on two verses from the Proverbs. Proverbs 3:5 states, "Trust in the LORD with all your heart and lean not on your own understanding." That is the truth God had vividly taught His people in the book of Leviticus. But Proverbs 14:12 describes the way the people actually responded, "There is a way that seems right to a man, but in the end it leads to death." Numbers is the record of the discipline of God in the lives of those whom He deeply loves and continually cares for, but who stubbornly resist Him, and thus delay their experience of victory and the joy of fellowship with a living God.

God's Provision (Numbers 1-10)

The book opens with God's command to take a census of the men 20 years old or more who were able to serve in the army. The Levites were omitted from the census because they were dedicated to the service of the tabernacle. Their place as the twelfth tribe was made up by dividing the tribe of Joseph into two tribes, named for Joseph's sons, Ephraim and Manasseh. Only those who had a clear pedigree could go forth to war. The lesson for the Christian is clear: only those who are certain they belong to the family of God can effectually do battle in the spiritual warfare to which we are called.

The camp is then set in order, with three tribes placed at each of the four points of the compass. The Levites gathered around the tabernacle, which was to be the center of everything in Israel's national life. Every person had an appointed place in the great army of Israel, just as each member of the body of Christ is placed according to the mind and will of God (see 1 Corinthians 12). Each of the families of Levi was assigned its special role in the work of caring for the tabernacle. The care given to the symbols of relationship with God suggests how important are His provisions for maintaining a strong spiritual life.

Chapter 7 deals with the voluntary offerings of the tribal leaders of Israel for the maintenance of worship. The fact that each identical offering was so carefully chronicled indicates the interest of God in each individual's gift. The Levites then appeared again, were separated from the rest of the people, cleansed, sprinkled, shaved, and finally presented to the Lord by Aaron. There is a clear analogy in this to the presentation of present-day believers before the Father by our great high priest, the Lord Jesus. He said of Himself, "For them I sanctify myself, that they too may be truly sanctified" (John 17:19). Thus we were separated by His death that we should be holy before God.

Three things yet remained to be set in order before the people began their march from Sinai. First, the Passover was kept for the first time after leaving Egypt. Second, the provision for guidance in the cloud and fire that rested over the tabernacle was made clear. The people were not responsible to determine either the time or the direction of their march, but were required only to be obedient to the signs from the Lord. Sometimes the cloud remained for two days, or a month, or even longer, and there was no option but to remain encamped. Surely, "Wait" is the hardest word to learn in the vocabulary of spiritual discipline. Finally, the people needed to learn the signals of the trumpets when they sounded.

The account closes with the call of Moses to invite the presence of the Lord, both at their setting out and at their resting, thus indicating that everything was centered in the presence and government of God.

The People's Rebellion (Numbers 11-25)

Chapters 11-25 record the people's discontent with God's provision and care. The first complaint was against the hardship of their circumstances. In response, fire from the Lord burned among them. Moses interceded on their behalf, and the fire abated. The next complaint arose over the monotonous diet of manna. All the people could think of were the varied foods of Egypt. They forgot the bondage and misery and remembered only Egypt's delights. God gave quail in such abundance that they ate them for an entire month—and then, as God predicted, they began to complain about the abundance of meat!

These rumblings of discontent were followed by a mutiny in Moses' own family. Aaron and Miriam complained about Moses' marriage to a Cushite woman, and expressed jealousy of his special relationship with God. Though the Lord directly explained to Aaron and Miriam that He had called Moses to a specialized ministry, nevertheless their jealousy continued, and Miriam was punished with leprosy. Upon the intercession of Moses, and after seven days' wait, Miriam was

---

1. This is an overview. You can study Numbers and Deuteronomy in more detail in Lessons 18-24 of the Joy of Living study, *Exodus: From Egypt to the Promised Land*

restored, for God is ever ready to pardon when evil is confessed and forsaken.

By this time the Israelites had reached the edge of the Promised Land. At God's command, 12 spies were chosen to enter the land and view both its resources and its dangers. After 40 days the men returned. Ten spies compared themselves with the giants (the Nephilim) and were disheartened, while two spies compared the giants with God and were greatly encouraged. Upon hearing the majority report, the people mutinied and took action to return to Egypt. Though Moses and Aaron fell face-down before the people, and Joshua and Caleb pleaded with them to act in faith rather than fear, the people responded by talking of stoning them.

At this God's patience was exhausted, and He threatened to cut them off and raise up another people through Moses. Once again Moses interceded for the people, pleading the honor of God and the gloating of the Egyptians should they hear that the Lord was unable to bring His people into the land of promise. Again it was God's grace working through His human instrument, Moses, as he pleaded for mercy.

The people were pardoned, but were sentenced to 40 years of wandering in the desert and to the exclusion from the land of everyone over 20 years of age. In a response of remorse rather than repentance, the people promised to go up to the land, and attempted to do so in spite of the warning that their day of opportunity was gone. A defeat at the hands of the Amalekites and Canaanites was the result.

Despite the Lord's warnings, rebellion continued to spread throughout the camp, and three men openly challenged the authority of Moses and Aaron. Korah, a Levite, resented the fact that the priesthood was confined to the family of Aaron; while Dathan and Abiram, both Reubenites, were contemptuous of Moses' authority and resentful of the circumstances into which he had brought them. Korah led 250 of the elders of Israel in offering priestly incense before the Lord. The cloud of glory appeared to the congregation, and the Lord warned all the assembly to stand back from the tents of Korah, Dathan, and Abiram. As these men and their families stood at the entrances of their tents, suddenly the ground opened beneath them and they were all swallowed alive. Furthermore, fire from the Lord consumed the 250 men who were offering the incense.

The next day the people again grumbled against Moses and Aaron, accusing them of being responsible for the deaths of those who had been punished. A plague from the Lord broke out among them, and 14,700 died before Aaron filled his censer with incense and fire from the altar and made atonement for the people. With that, the plague stopped. To make an end of the spirit of grumbling, God commanded each of the heads of Israel's tribes, including Aaron, to write his name upon a staff and leave it in the Tent of Meeting overnight. The next day Aaron's staff had budded, blossomed, and produced almonds, thus indicating that those who have the right to bear authority are those who walk in the fullness and fruitfulness of resurrection life.

Further regulations were then given for the sanctity of the priesthood and the work of the Levites, and provision was made for their support from tithes and offerings. The tribe of Levi was to have no part of the division of the land when they came into Canaan, for the tithe was to be their inheritance. The priests, likewise, were to have no inheritance, for the Lord Himself was their inheritance.

Special provision for cleansing from defilement was made. A red heifer was to be sacrificed, and its ashes were to be gathered, mixed with water, and used for certain cases of uncleanness, particularly those involved with touching dead bodies. Nothing could more graphically portray the contagiousness of sin. There is unavoidable defilement involved in contact with those "dead in…transgressions and sins" around us (Ephesians 2:1), and for this reason we must perpetually seek the fresh cleansing of the precious blood of Christ.

We now reach the record of events at the close of the 40 years, when the people were again at Kadesh. Here Miriam, the sister of Aaron and Moses, died and was buried. Also, once again the people were without water. When they complained, God graciously sent Moses and Aaron with the staff to a rock to speak to it, that the people might have water. But in irritation and unbelief Moses struck the rock twice. For this violation God told both Moses and Aaron that they would not be able to lead the people into the land. Nevertheless, he caused the rock to bring forth water for the people's needs.

Israel came to Mount Hor, and there Aaron died, after transferring his priestly garments to his son Eleazar. The king of Arad attacked Israel as they called upon the Lord for grace, and was defeated. Immediately after their victory came the incident of the venomous snakes sent among the people because of their grumbling against Moses. Jesus referred to this incident in His talk with Nicodemus (see John 3:14-15). Just as Moses lifted up a bronze likeness of the creature causing death, so Jesus, made in the likeness of sinful humanity, was lifted up to give life to all who would believe.

Chapters 22-24 tell the story of Balaam, a Gentile prophet who seemed to have a genuine knowledge of God, and yet whose heart was filled with greed. He was hired by Balak, the king of Moab, to curse Israel, since Moab was next on their route of conquest. Told by God that Israel was only to be blessed, Balaam sent the Moabite embassy home with his refusal. But once again Balak sent princes to him to offer a huge reward if he would come and curse Israel. Evidently God, reading the true intent of Balaam's heart, permitted him to go, though He was displeased with his motives. On the way, an angel of the Lord with drawn sword confronted Balaam. However, only Balaam's donkey saw the angel. Three times the donkey turned aside to avoid the avenging angel. But when Balaam, in anger, struck the donkey, the Lord opened the animal's mouth to rebuke the prophet.

Three times Balak sought to have Balaam curse Israel, and three times the prophet was unable to utter curses but instead predicted the sovereign call of Israel, their protection by God's hand, and their ultimate conquering of the peoples around. When the furious Balak refused to pay him, Balaam uttered an oracle of doom against Moab, Edom, the Amalekites, and the Kenites. In his final oracle he seemed to see even to the days of David, predicting, "A star will come out of Jacob; a scepter will rise out of Israel. He will crush the foreheads of Moab, the skulls of all the sons of Sheth" (Numbers 24:17). In its ultimate fulfillment this prophecy is fulfilled in the Messiah Himself.

God's Protection (Numbers 26-36)

A second census was taken of the men who were able to serve in the army. Instructions were then given to Moses concerning the division of the land when they came into Canaan. Of the original number that left Egypt, only two men were permitted to enter—Caleb and Joshua, the men of faith, who saw beyond the giants to the living God.

God informed Moses that the time had come for him to die, and at Moses' request for a successor, God appointed Joshua. Joshua would not inherit the full authority Moses exercised, but he would discover the Lord's will through the high priest by use of the Urim.

The book of Numbers closes where the last chapter of Deuteronomy begins, giving us the account of the actual death of Moses. Numbers is the record of the failure of the people in their perpetual stubbornness and foolishness, yet it is also the story of the unwearying patience and continual faithfulness of God. Thus it encourages those of us who have often found failure in our own spiritual life. We have come to learn, as the New Testament declares, "If we are faithless, he will remain faithful, for he cannot disown himself" (2 Timothy 2:13).

Deuteronomy

Deuteronomy, the last of the five books by Moses, is made up of three great sermons delivered by Moses shortly before his death. At this time the Israelites were made up of a new generation who were only children when their fathers had been given the law from Mount Sinai, and many of them were not yet even born at that time. Now they were about to enter the land of Canaan, and it was essential that they thoroughly understand their history before they made such a venture.

Review of the Journey (Deuteronomy 1-4)

In the first message, Moses reviewed the journey from the giving of the law at Mount Sinai (also called Mount Horeb) until the people reached their present location in the land of Moab at the edge of the Jordan River. Moses' first task was to recite to the people the wonderful love and care of God, who led them with the pillar of fire by night and the cloud by day, and guided them through the desert. He reminded them how God brought water from the rock to slake their thirst in a vast and waterless area, how He fed them with manna that did not fail, and how He delivered them from their enemies again and again, despite their unbelief.

In a note of pathos, Moses recalled his own eager desire to enter into the land when the people entered, but also God's denial of this to him, though he was permitted to view the land from the top of Mount Nebo. Moses closed with an exhortation to the people to remember the greatness of their God and to be obedient from their hearts. He warned also against the danger of idolatry, and reminded them of their surpassing privilege of relationship with the living God.

Second Giving of the Law (Deuteronomy 5-26)

The second message of Moses began with a fresh recital of the Ten Commandments as God gave them to Moses on Mount Sinai. It is from this that the book gets its name, for Deuteronomy means "the second (giving of) law." Deuteronomy is not merely a recital of

the journeys of Israel, but it is also the Lord's commentary upon the significance of those journeys and their events.

In connection with the giving of the law, Moses reminded the people that at that time they had promised to hear and to do all that God said. To this God had responded "Oh, that their hearts would be inclined to fear me and keep all my commands always, so that it might go well with them and their children for ever!" (Deuteronomy 5:29). Moses then proceeded to give them the famous Shemah, or "Hear, O Israel…" (Deuteronomy 6:4), which devout Jews have used for centuries to summarize the central feature of their faith—the uniqueness of their God. In connection with this was given God's requirement to observe these words, to teach them diligently to their children by means of talking to them when sitting in the house, walking by the way, lying down, or rising up. This is a great lesson on "teachable moments," when truth can be imparted more effectively than in formal situations.

Moses then began to review the conditions they would find in the land and the blessings that would await them there. He dealt with the danger Israel would face in confronting the corrupt nations already in the land. However tempted Israel might be to show mercy to them, they were commanded to thoroughly eliminate the inhabitants of Canaan, so that no vestige of their idolatries and depraved worship should remain to turn Israel aside from their worship of God. Israel was reminded that they were chosen because the Lord had set His love upon them, and that He Himself would be their strength in subjugating the nations of the land. Their own prosperity and good health would depend on the faithfulness by which they carried out these instructions. They need not fear the people of the land, for God Himself would cast them into great confusion until they were destroyed.

Moses recalled to the people the lessons God had taught them in the desert, how they had been humbled and fed with manna, so that they might know that "man does not live on bread alone but on every word that comes from the mouth of the Lord" (Deuteronomy 8:3). Jesus used these words to good effect against the tempter in the desert of Judea centuries later (see Matthew 4:4).

When the people had entered the land and were feasting upon its richness, they were to beware lest they begin to feel self-sufficient and to take credit in their own hearts for all that God had given them. They must not say to themselves that it was because of their own righteousness that the Lord brought them in; they must remember that they were a stubborn people, and that their history was one of continually provoking the Lord to wrath. Moses then recalled the awesome scene at Sinai, when, in the very face of the demonstration of the power and might of God, the people sinned by making the golden calf, and Moses had to intercede for them for 40 days and nights.

Moses reminded the people that God was not asking of them anything but to love Him and to serve Him with all their heart and soul, keeping His commandments and statutes for their own benefit. The central emphasis is that "the Lord your God is God of gods and Lord of lords, the great God, mighty and awesome" (Deuteronomy 10:17). Yet His actions toward them are those of infinite tenderness and love. As they entered the land, therefore, they were promised rain from heaven to water the earth, grass in the fields for their cattle, and power in their warfare to drive out great nations before them until the whole of the land would be their possession.

Chapters 12-21 constituted a series of statutes and ordinances, which were given to the people for their government within the land. They must first destroy all the places of worship of the nations then in the land, tearing down their altars and burning their Asherah poles. God would then indicate, in due season, one place within the land where they must bring their burnt offerings and sacrifices, and there they were to rejoice before the Lord. This was not fulfilled until the days of David and Solomon when the temple was built.

In Deuteronomy 18:15 a great promise was given, "The LORD your God will raise up for you a prophet like me from among your own brothers. You must listen to him." In some measure this prophecy was fulfilled by all the true prophets who would later rise in Israel, but it ultimately looked forward to the coming of Jesus (see Acts 3:22). It was Jesus who perfectly fulfilled the Old Testament ideal of priest, prophet, and king.

Chapters 22-26 gathered up various regulations for the life of the people within the land. The second message then concluded with instructions on how the people were to worship in the new land.

Revelation of the Future (Deuteronomy 27-31)

The third message of Moses was a great revelation of the future of Israel. Chapter 28 is one of the most amazing prophecies ever recorded, for it predicted the entire history of the Jewish people, even to the point where they ceased to be a nation and were scattered over the face of the earth.

Upon concluding his great prophecy, Moses reminded the people that on this day they stood before the Lord their God, and though there is much about His government which they could not fathom, nevertheless the things that had been revealed to them in their past were given that they might take heed to their present and walk faithfully before their God. In graphic and vivid terms he described to them what would result if they turned from the living God to the gods of the nations about them.

In his closing word, Moses seemed to look far into the future and see the people dispersed in lands of captivity. There he reminded them that if they would return to the Lord with all their heart and soul, God would forgive their sin, restore their fortunes, and gather them again into the land.

At this point, Moses uttered the great words which the apostle Paul quoted centuries later in his letter to the Romans, and which reveal the reason why Deuteronomy is called "the second law." Moses said to the people, "Now what I am commanding you today is not too difficult for you or beyond your reach" (Deuteronomy 30:11). This speaks of the Lord's provision by which the demands of the law might be fully met. "It is not necessary," Moses continued, "to go up to heaven and bring it down or to go beyond the sea and bring it back" (see verses 12-13), but as Moses put it very plainly, "The word is very near you; it is in your mouth and in your heart so that you may obey it" (Deuteronomy 30:14).

In Romans 10:5 Paul declared, "Moses describes in this way the righteousness that is by the law: 'The man who does these things will live by them.'" Here he quoted the words of Moses concerning the law given at Sinai and taken from the book of Exodus. Then in Romans 10:6-9 Paul quoted this very passage from Deuteronomy 30, declaring that it was not necessary to bring Christ down from heaven (the incarnation), or to bring Him up again from the dead (the resurrection), for this had already been done. It was only necessary that the heart believe and the lips confess that Jesus is Lord and risen from the dead. Thus "the second law," which Paul calls "the law of the Spirit of life" in Christ Jesus (Romans 8:2), fulfills by another principle the righteousness which the law demands.

Both of these principles were clearly taught to the people of Israel by Moses. He reiterated constantly the just demands of God expressed in the Ten Commandments. That was the first law. But, equally, he reminded them again and again of the gracious provision through the sacrifices and offerings to enable them to live at the level that God requires. The word "in your mouth" and "in your heart" would enable them to do all that God demanded.

Moses concluded his great address by saying, "See, I set before you today life and prosperity, death and destruction" (Deuteronomy 30:15). And with earnest words he pleaded with them to choose life "so that you and your children may live and that you may love the LORD your God, listen to his voice, and hold fast to him. For the LORD is your life, and he will give you many years in the land" (Deuteronomy 30:19-20).

In the final chapters, Moses summoned Joshua before him and charged him to be strong and courageous. Then God told Moses that the time had come for him to rest with his fathers, and that despite his faithful warnings, the people he had led would fulfill all his solemn predictions and God would necessarily visit them with the punishments announced.

Moses was then commanded to write a song, which would remain in the memory of the people long after Moses himself had departed. The song dealt with the great themes of God's everlasting covenant with Israel, His mercies to them, their failures and the penalties which followed, and the promise of final deliverance. Then before Moses' death he announced a benediction, concluding by reminding the people, "The eternal God is your refuge, and underneath are the everlasting arms" (Deuteronomy 33:27).

The final chapter recounts how Moses ascended Mount Nebo, and there he lay down and died, and the Lord Himself buried him in an unknown place in the valley of Moab.

Though the people immediately rallied around Joshua and gave to him the obedience which they had shown to Moses, they knew that they would never again see a man like Moses, to whom the Lord would speak face to face, and through whom He would manifest great and terrible deeds. It was not until the Messiah Himself would appear that the record of Moses would ever be excelled.

Study Questions

Before you begin your study this week:
- ❧ Pray and ask God to speak to you through His Holy Spirit.
- ❧ Use only the Bible for your answers.
- ❧ Write down your answers and the verses you used.
- ❧ Answer the "Challenge" questions if you have the time and want to do them.
- ❧ Share your answers to the "Personal" questions with the class only if you want to share them.

First Day: Read the Commentary on Numbers and Deuteronomy.

1. What meaningful or new thought did you find in the Commentary on Numbers and Deuteronomy, or from your teacher's lecture? What personal application did you choose to apply to your life?

2. Look for a verse in the lesson to memorize this week. Write it down, carry it with you, tack it to your bulletin board, on the dashboard of your car, etc. Make a real effort to learn the verse and its "address" (reference of where it is found in the Bible).

3. This week's questions focus on the book of Joshua. If you have time, you may want to read through the entire book this week. As you answer the questions, you will be looking up passages of Scripture from various places in the Bible. This will help you discover that God's Word is a "whole," and that His message to us is the same from Genesis to Revelation.

Second Day: Read Joshua 1:1-9.

The time had come for the people of Israel to enter into the land of promise. All those twenty years of age or older who had left Egypt some 40 years before had died in the desert, except for Caleb and Joshua. The new generation that had grown up during the desert journey had been fully instructed by Moses, prior to his death, in the laws and the sacrifices. At God's direction, Joshua had assumed the task of leading the people.

1. As the book of Joshua opens, the Israelites are camped on the east side of the Jordan River. From Joshua 1:1-2, what does God command Joshua and the Israelites to do?

2. a. From Joshua 1:3-4, what was God going to do for the Israelites?

   b. What encouragement did God give Joshua in Joshua 1:5?

3. a. What exhortation is repeated to Joshua in Joshua 1:6,7, and 9?

   b. What warning is given to Joshua in Joshua 1:7?

4. From Joshua 1:8, what is Joshua to do in order to be obedient to God? What would result in Joshua's life if he followed these instructions?

5. List each command God gives to Joshua in Joshua 1:9. Why is he able to obey them?

6. Personal: Do you have a daunting task or some humanly impossible situation set before you? Your situation is no different from Joshua's. If you are a believer, God has promised to be with you, too (see Matthew 28:20b). Write out Isaiah 41:10, personalizing it by inserting your name.

Third Day:

The Israelites were in the Promised Land, but it was only the beginning.

1. a. In preparation for Israel's conquest of the land, Joshua sent two spies into Jericho. Rahab, a prostitute, protected the spies and helped them escape. What do we learn about the people of the land from Rahab in Joshua 2:8-11?

    b. What does Rahab say in Joshua 2:9,12,13 that shows us that she believed and had faith in the Lord?

    c. Read Hebrews 11:31. What was the result of Rahab's faith?

    d. Challenge: What do you learn about Rahab from Matthew 1:5-16? (Summarize briefly.)

2. a. As we read in Deuteronomy 9, God was going to drive out the current inhabitants of the land because of their wickedness. From Joshua 3:5, what was the first step the Israelites were to take in preparation for their conquest?

    b. Read Joshua 5:2-7. After God miraculously parted the flooded Jordan River so that the Israelites could cross into the Promised Land on dry ground, what were the Israelites to do and why? (Summarize briefly.)

    c. Why was this important? Review Genesis 17:10-14 and summarize briefly.

3. a. Read Joshua 5:10-11. After healing from circumcision, what did the Israelites celebrate for the first time in the Promised Land?

    b. From Joshua 5:12, what major change took place in the lives of this new generation of Israelites?

4. a. Read Joshua 5:13—6:5. Note that God was not "taking sides." He had given the inhabitants of the land over 400 years to repent, and they had not; therefore, He was going to use Israel to remove them from the land. Rahab, an inhabitant of that land, obtained mercy because of her faith. From Joshua 6:3-5, summarize Israel's battle strategy.

    b. From Hebrews 11:30, how did the Israelites accomplish the overthrow of Jericho?

5. Rahab was spared because she acted in faith. The walls of Jericho fell because the Israelites, in faith, obeyed God. What does Hebrews 11:6 say regarding faith?

6. Personal: We are saved and cleansed from sin by God's grace, through faith (see Ephesians 2:8-9). Romans 5:1 tells us that we are called to the obedience that comes from faith. Take a moment to think of your own life. Do you really believe God? Does your life reflect the "obedience that comes from faith"? What are your thoughts on this?

Fourth Day:

1. a. After experiencing defeat because of sin within the camp, then dealing with that sin and again being given victory, the Israelites renewed their covenant with God at Mt. Ebal. The Canaanite kings west of the Jordan River came together to stop the Israelites' conquest. However the people of Gibeon, afraid for their lives, resorted to a ruse. The Gibeonites pretended their homes were far away, so far that their provisions, which had been fresh when they began their journey, were now stale. What mistake did the Israelites make in Joshua 9:14?

   b. What was the result of Gibeon's deception? (Joshua 9:15)

2. Read Joshua 10:1-6. What was the result of the treaty? (Summarize briefly.)

3. Read Joshua 10:7-14 and summarize how God used the threat.

4. Having conquered the central part of the Promised Land, Joshua then turned toward the southern portion. Summarize what Joshua 10:40-42 says regarding this campaign.

5. a. Read Joshua 11:1-5. What happened when Jabin king of Hazor heard of these victories? (Summarize briefly.)

   b. From Joshua 11:7-9, what was the outcome?

6. Joshua waged war for a long time. Read Joshua 11:19-20. Except for the Gibeonites, why did no one seek a peace treaty?

7 Personal: So often people see great wickedness and say, "Why doesn't God do something?" Then when He does, they can't understand. God, in mercy, had given the people of Canaan 400 years to repent, but they did not. Their iniquity had reached its full measure (see Genesis 15:16), and the Israelites were God's hand of judgment. To each one of us there is a period of time given to repent and turn to God. Tomorrow is not promised to us. He says, "I tell you, now is the time of God's favor, now is the day of salvation" (2 Corinthians 6:2b). Have you repented of your sin and trusted in Jesus Christ for your salvation? If not, will you do it now?

Fifth Day: Read Joshua 14:2-5.

After seven years of conflict much of the land had been conquered. However, there were still very large areas to be taken over. God instructed Joshua, now an old man, to divide the land among the tribes.

1. Read Joshua 14:2-3. How was the land divided among nine and a half of the tribes? How did two and a half tribes receive their inheritance?'

2. a. When counting, it sometimes appears there are 13 tribes listed, yet there are only twelve tribes of Israel. From Joshua 14:4a, what happened to the tribe of Joseph to cause this?

   b. Challenge: Read Genesis 48:5-6, and explain when and how these half-tribes began.

3. Compare Joshua 14:4b with Numbers 18:20-21. What tribe was not allotted a portion of the land? Describe that tribe's inheritance and God's provision for them.

4. Read Joshua 18:1. What was set up at Shiloh?

5. The best land was not purchased by the richest tribes, nor taken by force by the mightiest tribes. The land was divided fairly among the tribes by lot. What does Proverbs 16:33 say regarding the casting of the lot?

6. Personal: The land God gave to each tribe was different, and each tribe had different enemies to drive out before they completely possessed the land, but all the land held blessing for His people. The difficulties we each face are different, but God has blessing for each of His children. Will you trust God to help you with the difficulties you face in life, and rejoice in the blessings He has given you? Make a list of at least five blessings God has given to you. Now take a moment and thank Him for each one.

Sixth Day: Read Joshua 23-24.

Joshua was now nearing the age of 110. The Lord had given Israel, as a whole, rest from their enemies around them, although there were still battles to be fought by individual tribes or groupings of tribes.

1. a. Joshua 23 is Joshua's farewell to the leaders of Israel. After reminding them of all that God had done for them, what did Joshua say they should do in verses 6 and 8?

   b. What did he say they shouldn't do in verse 7?

2. From Joshua 23:14-16, just as God had fulfilled all His promises for good to the Israelites, He would also fulfill all He threatened to do if the Israelites did what?

3. a. Joshua then gathered all Israel together at Shechem, where they had previously made a covenant to serve the Lord. As he prepared to die, he wanted the Israelites to renew their covenant with the Lord. After reminding them of all that God had done for them, what did he exhort them to do? (Joshua 24:14-15)

   b. Summarize their response. (Joshua 24:16-18)

   c. What was set up as a witness to all that was said? (Joshua 24:26-27)

4. After sending the people back to their homes, Joshua died and was buried. From Joshua 24:31, how long did the Israelites serve the Lord?

5. a. Read Genesis 50:25, which took place in Egypt nearly five hundred years earlier. What did Joseph know that God would do, and what promise did he extract from his brothers?

   b. How was this brought to completion in Joshua 24:32?

6. Personal: All of God's promises are true, and He will fulfill them—in His time and His way. Our walk in this life is not always easy, and there are battles of faith to be fought. Either we trust God or we don't. Read Hebrews 10:35-36, and write down what God is speaking to your heart. You may choose to personalize these verses by inserting your own name.

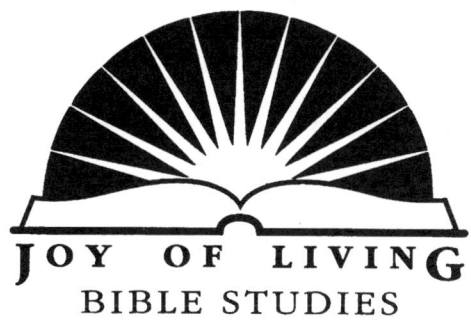

Joshua — The Way to Victory

The time had come for the people of Israel to enter into the land of promise. All those who left Egypt some 40 years before had died in the desert, except for Caleb and Joshua. A new generation had grown up during the desert journey. Moses had fully instructed them in the laws and the sacrifices before he died, and Joshua had assumed the task of leading the people into the land.

Moses, the great lawgiver, was not permitted to take the people into the fulfillment of promise; rather, Joshua (whose Hebrew name is the equivalent of the Greek name, Jesus) is given that privilege. This is surely an anticipation of the New Testament truth that the law cannot fulfill the promises of God, but they are all available to us through our heavenly commander, Jesus.

Nevertheless, Joshua was instructed in the use of the law as necessary for meditation and as a guideline to obedience. But the strength by which the promise would be fulfilled lay in the great word, "Be strong and courageous. Do not be terrified; do not be discouraged, for the LORD your God will be with you wherever you go" (Joshua 1:9).

Victory Is Possible (Joshua 1-11)

After reminding the tribes of Reuben and Gad and the half tribe of Manasseh of their promise to assist their relatives in the conquest of the land, Joshua sent out his spies to view the situation. These went out as he himself had gone out 38 years before, in confidence and faith that God intended to give them the land.

With boldness they entered the city of Jericho and were hidden in the house of Rahab, a prostitute, who informed them that the people were afraid of the Israelites, having heard of their miraculous deliverance at the Red Sea and their conquest of the two Amorite kings, Sihon and Og. The very people which Israel had feared at Kadesh-Barnea were themselves now afraid of Israel! Rahab's personal confidence that the God of Israel was the Lord of all the earth led her to hide the two spies and aid in their subsequent escape from the city, after having them promise that when the city fell she and her household would be spared.

Forsake Unbelief

After the spies returned, Joshua ordered the people to assemble for the crossing of the Jordan. The Ark of the Covenant leading the way would show the people that a living God was among them as He opened a way through the Jordan, just as He had once opened a way through the Red Sea.

Twelve men were chosen, one from each tribe, to memorialize the occasion. As the feet of the priests touched the edge of the Jordan, the waters began to recede, having been cut off far upstream near the little city of Adam.

The priests bearing the Ark of the Covenant remained in the middle of the river until all the people passed through. Then a monument of 12 stones carried from the middle of the river by the twelve men was built at the river's edge. These were to be a memorial for the children to see, that they might ask and receive an explanation from their parents.

As we seek the significance of this event in the Christian life, we must remember that just as the crossing of the Red Sea meant the willingness to forsake the world pictured by Egypt, so the crossing of the Jordan indicates a willingness to enter into all the promises which God has given the believer in Jesus Christ. It acknowledges the choice to forsake the unbelief of the desert and to fully lay hold of all that God has made available.

Depend on God

Four significant events are recorded in chapter 5. First, all the males of Israel were circumcised at Gilgal. The name means "rolling away," for here the Lord said Israel had "rolled away the reproach of Egypt" (Joshua 5:9). Evidently the nation had forsaken this ritual during the desert wanderings; thus the mark of difference between them and the pagan nations around them had disappeared. Before the land was conquered they must again be seen as the distinct people of God. The New Testament speaks of a "circumcision of the heart" (Romans 2:29), which is the counterpart to this Old Testament ritual and indicates a heart that is ready to forsake all dependence on the natural life and rely upon the strength of God alone.

The second event in Gilgal was the celebration of the Passover for only the second time since leaving Egypt. Then the day after the Passover the provision of manna ceased entirely, the third event of this chapter, and the people began to subsist upon the natural produce of the land of Canaan. This corresponds to our spiritual feeding upon the full potential of the resources we have in Christ.

The fourth event of chapter 5 was Joshua's encounter with the commander of the army of the Lord. Clearly it was not up to Joshua to plan the strategy of this campaign of conquest, but God Himself would do so, just as today it is not the church's task to develop the strategy by which it can overcome the world, but it is to obey the Word of the Lord and to obey the pattern of the church's function as given in the New Testament.

Obey God's Direction

Both the foolishness of the Jericho strategy in the eyes of the watching world, and God's mighty power to conquer were revealed in the subsequent actions of Israel. Upon reaching the city of Jericho with its massive walls, the people were instructed to march once around the city in silence while the priests sounded trumpets. Each day for six days this was Joshua's command. Then on the seventh day the people were told to circle the city seven times, and, when the priests blew a mighty blast of the trumpets, the people were to shout, and the walls would fall down.

The people had faith enough to obey this apparently foolish plan. And on the seventh day, exactly as predicted, the mighty walls tumbled down at their shout of faith. Rahab and her family were spared according to the prearranged provision, but the city was sacked, and the rest of the inhabitants were put to the sword. Joshua pronounced a curse, involving the death of the firstborn and of the youngest son of any who would rebuild the city. The fulfillment of this curse some two hundred years later is recorded in 1 Kings 16:34.

As Christians we must not rely on our own wisdom or strength to triumph in our spiritual battles, but instead we must seek God's direction and fight the "good fight of the faith" (1 Timothy 6:12), acting in obedience to His direction.

Battle the Sinful Nature

Chapters 7 and 8 give us the bittersweet story of Ai, the next city in the line of conquest. It was such a small city and looked so easy to overcome that only a few thousand were sent to capture it. They suffered, however, a serious defeat, and about 36 Israelites were killed. As Joshua inquired before the Lord the reason for this, God told him that the defeat resulted from an incomplete obedience within the camp of Israel: one man, Achan, of the tribe of Judah, had disobeyed the instructions concerning Jericho, and had hidden in his tent some silver, a wedge of gold, and a beautiful robe from Babylonia.

This helps us understand the symbolic significance of Ai in our own lives. It is a picture of the sinful nature within us, inherited from Adam, which also loves the things of the world, and yet it appears to us to be of little consequence and easily overcome.

When the sin of Achan was discovered, apparently by the casting of lots, the seemingly harsh but faithful judging of the people by stoning Achan to death made possible a renewed attack upon the city of Ai, this time by the strategy of ambush. The city fell, and all the inhabitants were put to the sword. Thus it is evident that the conquest of our enemy, the sinful nature within, is accomplished by our willingness to accept the judgment of death upon it, and to take up battle against it by the power of the Spirit, "for the sinful nature desires what is contrary to the Spirit, and the Spirit what is contrary to the sinful nature" (Galatians 5:17).

Since Ai was the gateway to the west, its defeat left the entire central portion of the land of promise open to the Israelites. Joshua's first act was to fulfill the command of Moses and to build an altar upon Mount Ebal. There, as the law had carefully provided, the blessings were read from Mount Gerizim and the cursings from Mount Ebal, that Israel (and we) should forever remember the blessings that will follow the putting aside of the sinful nature and the cursings which will inevitably appear if we fail to accept the judgment of the cross upon our natural life.

Resist the Devil

The kings of the west along the coastal plain from Gaza in the south to Lebanon in the north met together to form a league to stop the Israelites' conquest. One of the cities that lay in the immediate path of Joshua and his armies was Gibeon, near present-day Jerusalem. Afraid for their lives, the Gibeonites resorted to a ruse to trick the Israelites into making a treaty of peace with them—a treaty which God had strictly forbidden to be made with any of the inhabitants of the land. When Joshua later learned of their deceit, the worst he could do to them was to make them woodcutters and water-carriers for Israel.

The kings of the Canaanite cities to the south now determined to combine their armies for a united attack on Gibeon. Thus attacked, Gibeon immediately called upon Joshua for defense, in accordance with the treaty of peace he had made with them. Marching from Gilgal at God's direction, Joshua and his armies traveled by night and took the enemy armies by surprise, throwing them into a panic. It was on this great occasion that Joshua prayed and asked for the lengthening of the day, that they might have enough time to defeat the enemy. It is recorded that the sun stood still over Gibeon and the moon over the valley of Aijalon for about a full day. Accompanying this, large hailstones fell from the sky, killing even more of the allied armies than the swords of the Israelites.

Symbolically, this account pictures the ability of Satan to use circumstances in such a way as to harass and frighten the Christian, but when such circumstances are met by the resolute heart of faith, the very circumstances are turned to the benefit of the believer.

Obey the Living God

After the battle of Gibeon, the conquest of the south was soon accomplished. The cities were taken one by one, and the inhabitants were slaughtered in obedience to the command of God to eliminate the Canaanites in their entirety. Then the kings in the northern part of Canaan banded together under the leadership of King Jabin of the city of Hazor. Joshua met them in battle at the waters of Merom, and another great victory was accomplished, including the taking of Hazor.

With the defeat of the northern kings, the entire land lay under the control of Israel. God's promise to Joshua that "no one will be able to stand up against you" (Joshua 1:5) had been fulfilled. Thus we see the enemies of the believer are overcome by means of faith and obedience to the Word of the living God.

This first section of the book of Joshua helps us understand that victory is possible over the world, the sinful nature, and the devil (see Ephesians 2). And though there may be temporary failures (as at Ai) and partial compromises (as with the Gibeonites), God will give us victory.

The Conquests (Joshua 12-21)

The second section of the book primarily consists of a listing of the enemies who were subdued under Joshua's first attack, in the first seven years after Israel had entered the land. Then we learn how the land was apportioned bit by bit to the various tribes according to the casting of lots. This device permitted the decision to be according to God's plan and not according to human wisdom. Thus each tribe would know that the portion of land given to them was given by God's own choice. We are reminded today that the circumstances in which we find ourselves are not necessarily of our own choosing, but the hand of the Lord has brought us to the place where, for the present at least, we are to be.

Though the major portion of the land promised to Abraham was now under Israel's control, along the fringes there were still unoccupied territories, and within the land itself pockets of resistance remained. When Joshua allotted each tribe its own territory by casting lots, he reminded them that they were individually responsible to claim the territory which rightly belonged to them. There would be battles involved, but they were assured that the ultimate victory would be secure, for God had given His promise.

Scattered within this section are isolated stories which constitute beautiful illustrations of personal faith. One is the story of Caleb, who at 85 years of age was still willing to claim the inheritance promised to him when he was in the desert with Moses. In accordance with his request, Caleb was allotted the city of Hebron and its provinces as a permanent inheritance. But in order to conquer it he had to drive out the "giants" (Anakites) who lived there.

This section also gives the account of the setting up of the tabernacle at the city of Shiloh, the allotment of an inheritance to the daughters of Zelophehad as Moses had promised them, and the designation of cities of refuge as the law had provided. The Levites, of course, were given no inheritance within the land except for certain cities to live in, and they were reminded again that the Lord was their inheritance. As previously seen, the tribes of Reuben and Gad and the half-tribe of Manasseh were given their part on the east of the Jordan, but the rest of the land was divided between the nine and one-half tribes.

The Consecration (Joshua 22-24)

The last portion of the book of Joshua includes the account of the misunderstanding which arose regarding the tribes of Reuben and Gad and the half-tribe of Manasseh east of the Jordan, and closes with two addresses by Joshua to the people shortly before his death. When the major portion of the land had been conquered, Joshua permitted the two and one-half tribes to return to their homes east of the Jordan, but to the dismay of the other nine and one-half tribes, the eastern Israelites immediately erected an altar on the west side of the river.

Remembering the sin of Achan and how God had punished the whole nation for the sin of one man, the western tribes gathered armies at Shiloh, under the leadership of Phinehas. They came to Gilead and demanded an explanation, reminding the eastern tribes that offerings and sacrifices were to be offered only at the tabernacle in Shiloh.

The two and one-half tribes then explained that they had no intention of using the altar for any such sacrifices, but had erected it as a memorial to teach their children that they too shared the inheritance of the Lord with the rest of Israel.

Aware of his advanced age, and knowing he would soon die, Joshua summoned Israel to Shechem, and there he delivered two magnificent addresses which close the book. The first was a warning against turning to the idolatry of the surrounding nations, and a solemn promise that if they did so, God would permit them to fall again under the power of their enemies. The second address was a marvelous review of the way the Lord had led them, from the plagues of Egypt to the conquest of the Promised Land. Joshua ended his message with a magnificent summons to the people to make a personal choice among themselves as to whom they would serve, but he warned again that such service must be from the heart and not from lips only.

Shortly after having recorded the promise of the people to serve the Lord, Joshua died at the age of 110. The close of this book looks back to the close of Genesis and records how the bones of Joseph were at last buried in the city of Shechem, in the ground which Jacob had bought from the Hittites. Thus, in the words appearing on the memorial to John Wesley in Westminster Abbey, "God buries His workmen but carries on His work."

Study Questions

Before you begin your study this week:

- ❧ Pray and ask God to speak to you through His Holy Spirit.
- ❧ Use only the Bible for your answers.
- ❧ Write down your answers and the verses you used.
- ❧ Answer the "Challenge" questions if you have the time and want to do them.
- ❧ Share your answers to the "Personal" questions with the class only if you want to share them.

First Day: Read the Commentary on Joshua.

1. What meaningful or new thought did you find in the Commentary on Joshua, or from your teacher's lecture? What personal application did you choose to apply to your life?

2. Look for a verse in the lesson to memorize this week. Write it down, carry it with you, tack it to your bulletin board, on the dashboard of your car, etc. Make a real effort to learn the verse and its "address" (reference of where it is found in the Bible).

3. This week's questions focus on the books of Judges and Ruth. If you have time, you may want to read through both books this week. As you answer the questions, you will be looking up passages of Scripture from various places in the Bible. This will help you discover that God's Word is a "whole," and that His message to us is the same from Genesis to Revelation.

The book of Judges relates the history of Israel between the days immediately following Joshua's death and the time of the prophet Samuel, when the first king over all of Israel was chosen. The events are not written in chronological order with one judge following after another. Some events may have taken place simultaneously in various parts of Israel.

Second Day:

1. In Deuteronomy 7:1-2 God had promised to bring the Israelites into the Promised Land, drive out the nations before them, and deliver those nations over to Israel. In response, what were Israel's responsibilities? (verses 3-5)

2. After the death of Joshua and of the generation that had personally experienced the reality of God, Israel began a cycle that was repeated many times throughout the book of Judges. List the steps or actions you see in each of the following passages.

   Judges 2:11-13

   Judges 2:14-15

   Judges 2:16,18

   Judges 2:17,19

3. Read Judges 2:20. Why was God angry with Israel?

4. a. Read Judges 2:21-22. What judgment did God pronounce on Israel and to what purpose?

    b. Read Judges 3:6-7. How did the Israelites respond to the presence of these nations?

5. It is easy to read about the Israelites and their actions and wonder how they could so easily disobey God and fall into sin. What warnings does God give us in the following verses?

    1 Corinthians 10:12-13

    1 Peter 5: 8

    Hebrews 2:1

6. Personal: It is easy to recognize and judge sin in the lives of others, but not so easy to recognize it in ourselves. Take a few moments to pray and ask God to help you recognize the sin in your life, including an attitude of condemnation toward others. Ask Him to help you to always be alert to your reactions and to your attitudes.

Third Day:

1. a. Read Judges 3:9-11. When the Israelites forgot the Lord and worshipped other gods, He allowed them to fall under the rule of Aram. What prompted the Lord to raise up a deliverer? (verse 9a)

    b. Who was the deliverer that God raised up? (verse 9b)

    c. How long did Israel have peace? (verse 11)

2. a. Read Judges 3:15-30. After Othniel's death, the people again did evil in the eyes of the Lord and He gave Eglon, king of Moab, power over Israel. What prompted the Lord to raise up a deliverer? (verse 15)

    b. How long did Israel have peace? (verse 30)

3. a. Read Judges 4:3-9. After Ehud died, the Israelites again did evil in the eyes of the Lord, so the Lord sold them into the hands of Jabin, a king of Canaan, who made life unbearable for them for 20 years. What prompted the Lord to raise up a deliverer? (verse 3)

    b. Through whom did God send a command to Barak? (verses 4-7)

    c. On what condition would Barak go? (verse 8)

    d. Because of this, to whom would God deliver Sisera, the commander of Jabin's army? (verse 9)

4. a. Read Judges 4:14-21 and 5:31. Upon hearing of Barak's action, Sisera gathered his chariots. Who routed Sisera? (4:14-15)

   b. Whom did God use to kill Sisera? (4:21)

   c. How long did Israel have peace? (5:31)

5. Personal: It is amazing the number of times God forgave the Israelites when they asked for His forgiveness. Is there someone you have difficulty forgiving? What does Matthew 18:21-22 say? This is not always easy. If you are having trouble forgiving someone, confess this to God and ask Him to change your heart.

Fourth Day:

The 40 years of peace that followed was broken once again by the idolatry of Israel. This time it was the people of Midian who for seven years so harassed the Israelites that they were reduced to living in caves.

1. a. Read Judges 6:7-16. What prompted the Lord to action? (verse 7)

   b. Although the Lord sent a prophet to rebuke Israel, whom did He call to be a judge, and how did He call this man? (verses 11-12)

   c. What questions did Gideon ask? (verse 13)

   d. Why did Gideon doubt that God could use him? (verses 14-15)

   e. What assurance did God give him? (verse 16)

2. At God's command Gideon reduced his fighting men from 30,000 to 300. Although he trusted the Lord and was acting in obedience, Gideon still struggled with doubt. From the following passages, how did God build Gideon's faith? (summarize briefly)

   Judges 6:36-40

   Judges 7:9-15

3. By acting in obedience to God's instruction, Israel defeated Midian. From Judges 8:28, how long did Israel enjoy peace?

4. Personal: Just because you are a Christian does not mean you'll never have times of doubt. Thankfully, God has given us a record of others, like Gideon, who have believed yet struggled to trust, and God still helped them. Are you having trouble trusting God in some area of your life? Won't you pray the prayer of a boy's father in Mark 9:24?

Fifth Day:

1. And so the cycle continued. No sooner had Gideon died than the Israelites again prostituted themselves to the Baals, but in time God sent two judges, Tola and Jair. Read Judges 10:1-3. How many years did each lead Israel?

2. After these judges died, Israel again did evil in the eyes of the Lord, and He allowed the Philistines and the Ammonites to oppress them for 18 years. As before, when they repented and turned to the Lord. He raised up judges to deliver and lead them. Read Judges 11:32 and 12:7. Who was the judge that delivered Israel from the Ammonites, and how long did he lead Israel?

3. After the death of Jephthah, a series of three little-known judges, Ibzan, Elon, and Abdon, arose in various parts of Israel. Read Judges 12:8-15. How long did they each lead Israel?

4. a. Yet Israel again did evil in the eyes of the Lord, and they were delivered into the hands of the Philistines for forty years. Read Judges 13:2-5. What is different about the calling of this judge and what he would do?

   b. When Samson grew to manhood, he manifested the presence of the Spirit of the Lord in deeds of great physical strength. His one weakness seemed to stem from an attraction to the daughters of the Philistines. His relationships with them led to altercations with and small triumphs over the Philistines, but also to his downfall. Read Judges 16:20-21. What resulted from Samson's repeatedly giving way to his weakness and eventually revealing the source of his strength?

   c. Even in prison God's grace did not forsake Samson, His chosen servant. Summarize what happened in Judges 16:25-30.

5. Personal: God's mighty man, wretched and blinded, reminds us to "abstain from sinful desires, which war against your soul" (1 Peter 2:11). Left unjudged, sinful desires will bring the mightiest saint into bondage and darkness. Samson's life testifies that even those of great spiritual ability can fall from their place of usefulness. Although God in His faithfulness will not desert them, their spiritual effectiveness is far from what it could have been. Is there some sin that you refuse to give up or that you somehow justify, even though the Holy Spirit keeps tugging at your heart? What are you going to do about it?

Sixth Day:

We must remember that no matter how evil the time, God always has those who love Him and seek to obey Him.

1. The strange stories in Judges 17-21 are apparently included that we may have a picture of the ignorance and evil which were manifested among the Israelites when they repeatedly turned from the living God. Read Judges 17:6 and 21:25. Instead of obeying God, what did the Israelites do?

2. a. The story of Ruth takes place during the spiritually dark days of the judges. Read Ruth 1:1-5. What problem existed in the land of Judah? What did Elimelech do to provide for his family? (verses 1-2)

    b. While there, what did Elimelech's sons do? (verse 4a)

    c. What happened to Elimelech and his sons? (verses 3, 4b-5)

3. When Naomi learned there was food in Bethlehem, she decided to return home. What did she tell her daughters-in-law, and how did they respond? (Ruth 1:6-18; summarize briefly)

4. a. Read Ruth 2:1-12. When Naomi and Ruth arrived in Bethlehem, how did they obtain food? (verse 2)

    b. Whose field did she work in, and what benefits did this bring? (verses 1, 3-9, summarize briefly)

    c. Where had Ruth taken refuge? (verses 10-12)

5. a. Read Ruth 4:13-17. What eventually happened to Boaz, Ruth and Naomi? (verses 13-16)

    b. What famous person was the descendant of this child? (verse 17)

    c. Read Matthew 1:1. Who else was their descendant?

6. Personal: There are so many lessons to learn from the books of Judges and Ruth. List one or two truths or lessons that really stood out to you.

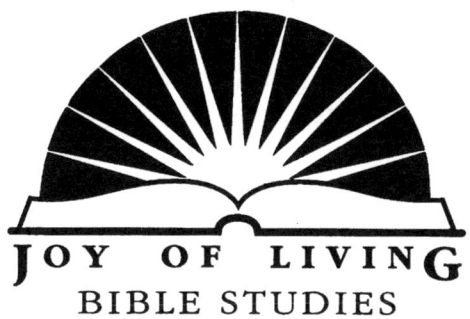

Judges & Ruth — The Incomplete Victory[1]

The book of Judges relates the history of Israel between the days of Joshua and the time of the prophet Samuel, when the first king over all of Israel was chosen. It takes its name from the series of judges God raised up to deliver the people when they had fallen into the hands of their enemies. The repeated theme of the book is stated first in Judges 2:18-19: "Whenever the LORD raised up a judge for them, he was with the judge and saved them out of the hands of their enemies as long as the judge lived; for the LORD had compassion on them as they groaned under those who oppressed and afflicted them. But when the judge died, the people returned to ways even more corrupt than those of their fathers, following other gods and serving and worshipping them. They refused to give up their evil practices and stubborn ways."

Israel's Failure

Judges 1-2 reviews the situation in Israel after the death of Joshua. Though Judah and Simeon subdued the Canaanites within their territory, some areas, especially the Philistine cities of the coast, remained unconquered. Benjamin, Manasseh, Zebulun, and Dan also failed to fully conquer the peoples within their allotted borders.

So once again the angel of the Lord appeared to warn the people of the inevitable consequences of their unbelief and incomplete obedience. Though the people of Israel wept and apparently repented, their repentance was not long lived. Soon they were again bowing before the idols of neighboring nations. Parallel to this in the Christian's life is the continual temptation to adopt the goals and standards of the world, and to seek the favor and approval of men rather than of God.

Judges 3 says that God used the remaining Canaanite tribes to teach the new generation within Israel how to make war—that is, how God, rather than people, makes war. As Paul said in 2 Corinthians 10:4, "The weapons we fight with are not the weapons of the world. On the contrary, they have divine power to demolish strongholds."

A Succession of Judges

When Israel fell into idolatry, God allowed them to be conquered by the nations around them. They first fell under the rule of Aram, but when they repented, Caleb's nephew Othniel led the forces of Israel

1. This is an overview. You can study Judges and Ruth in more detail in the Joy of Living study titled *Judges & Ruth*.

to drive Aram from the land. For 40 years he ruled as the first judge of Israel, and the land had peace during that time.

After Othniel's death, the people again fell into sinful ways, and God allowed Moab to conquer a part of Israel. For 18 years the Moabites held the people in bondage, requiring heavy tribute from them. At last the people wearied of their bondage and turned again to the Lord. In gracious response He raised up Ehud from the tribe of Benjamin, who was chosen to carry the tribute to Moab. There he tricked the king into receiving him in private, and when the two were alone, Ehud drew a sword and thrust it into the king's belly. Then Ehud returned to Israel and mustered an army large enough to attack the Moabites, eventually killing about 10,000 of their best warriors.

The land again enjoyed peace for about 40 years under Ehud, and apparently another 40 years under Shamgar, who gained fame for killing 600 Philistines with an ox-goad. (It should be noted that the periods of relief under the judges are not to be taken consecutively, for some of them overlap, there being one judge ruling in one part of the country and another ruling in another part.)

Deborah (Judges 4-5)

In the north, the Israelites fell under the hand of Jabin, king of Hazor, who made life unbearable for Israel for 20 years. The leader of faith in that part of Israel was a woman named Deborah, who judged Israel in the hill country of Ephraim. Through her God sent a command to Barak from the tribe of Naphtali to lead 10,000 men against Jabin. Barak refused to go to battle unless Deborah went with him. When she consented, 10,000 men assembled on the slopes of Mount Tabor and prepared to assault the army of Jabin, led by his general Sisera.

The Canaanite army panicked before Israel. Sisera fled on foot and found what he thought to be a refuge in the tent of a woman named Jael. While Sisera slept, Jael took an iron tent peg and a hammer and drove the long spike through Sisera's head, ending both his life and the power of the northern Canaanite tribes.

This use of two women, Deborah and Jael, confirms the statement in Galatians 3:28 that in Christ "there is neither...male nor female." Deborah fulfilled the office of prophet, while Jael was an instrument in the hand of the Lord to remove the enemies of Israel.

Gideon (Judges 6-9)

The 40 years of peace that followed was broken once again by the faithless idolatry of Israel. This time it was the people of Midian who for seven years so harassed the Israelites that they were reduced to living in caves. They claimed all the Israelites' livestock for themselves, and stripped the land of its fodder by enormous herds of camels.

Again Israel's deep trouble brought about their repentant cry for help, but they were warned by a prophet of God that their situation was merely a fulfillment of what the Lord had predicted many years before through Moses. Nevertheless, in grace, God sent the angel of the Lord to appear to Gideon, who was threshing wheat in a winepress to hide it from the Midianites. Gideon stated his low status in the nation as his reason for being unable to lead Israel to overthrow Midian.

God reassured him with, "I will be with you" (Judges 6:16), and Gideon returned to his home to prepare a meal for his visitor. When Gideon spread the meat and bread upon a rock, the angel touched it with his staff, and the fire of the Lord consumed the sacrifice. That night Gideon pulled down the altar to Baal and the Asherah pole. When his neighbors discovered what he had done, they threatened to kill him for insulting their god, but Gideon's father Joash defended his son by arguing that if Baal was truly a god, he could defend himself.

Soon after, the armies of Midian and other neighboring nations joined forces against Israel. God graciously strengthened Gideon's faith by twice giving him a miraculous sign involving the fleece of a sheep. So Gideon gathered 32,000 men of the northern tribes and assembled them at the foot of Mount Gilead. Across the valley, the Midianite hosts were as numerous as a plague of locusts, but the Lord told Gideon that he had too many men. God wanted to be sure that Israel knew who would defeat the Midianites. When Gideon had sent home all the fainthearted, there were still 10,000 men of Israel left. Again, at the Lord's command, Gideon tested them at the water, and only 300 men remained.

Gideon's faith was strengthened when, at God's suggestion, he went down to the Midianite camp in the darkness. He heard a man of Midian recounting a dream. The other soldier interpreted it as an omen of the defeat of Midian, and when Gideon heard it, he breathed a prayer of worship to God there on the spot.

Putting torches within large pottery jars, and carrying trumpets and swords, the 300 Israelites divided into three groups and surrounded the Midianite camp. Shortly after midnight, Gideon gave the signal and his men broke the jars, causing the torches to flash out, and sounded the trumpets. Then they watched the Midianite army destroy itself, as God caused the Midianites to turn on each other. In their confusion and panic the Midianites fled. The waiting Israelite troops of Naphtali, Asher and Manasseh then joined the fight, chasing the retreating Midianites, and capturing and killing their two generals.

Gideon refused the request of Israel to make him king, but foolishly he made a priest's garment for himself out of the gold that came from the earrings of the Midianites. This soon became an object of idolatrous worship by Israel. But the land again had peace for 40 years while Gideon judged the nation.

Two judges next appear briefly. One was named Tola, from the tribe of Issachar, who judged for 23 years. He was succeeded by Jair from Gilead, who judged Israel for 22 years. Then, as before, the people of Israel turned away from the Lord to worship pagan gods. Because they had ceased worshipping God, it was not long before the Philistines and Ammonites were again tormenting Israel.

Jephthah (Judges 10-12)

After 18 years, the Israelites pleaded for deliverance. In an amazing display of grace, when they had at last put away foreign gods, the heart of God grieved over their misery. When the Ammonites launched an attack against Israel, God laid hold of Jephthah, the son of a prostitute. Jephthah's brothers had driven him away from their home, that he might not share the inheritance with them. Under pressure of the Ammonite advance, the elders of Gilead, Jephthah's brothers, sent to him and asked him to lead the Israelites against Ammon.

Before the battle, Jephthah vowed to the Lord that he would offer in sacrifice whatever or whoever came out of his house to greet him on his return. Thus after the rout of the Ammonites, Jephthah returned, and his daughter met him at the door. Jephthah refused to break his vow, and "he did to her as he had vowed" (Judges 11:39). This story has been the subject of much debate among scholars. Did he actually sacrifice her, or not? Since we have seen in Exodus that a provision was made to redeem all firstborn sons—who also were vowed to the Lord—by the payment of redemption money, it is possible that this was done in this case also.

After the death of Jephthah, a series of three little-known judges, Ibzan, Elon, and Abdon, arose in various parts of Israel, judging for periods of seven to ten years each.

Samson (Judges 13-16)

Israel again did evil in the eyes of the Lord, which resulted in oppression by the Philistines. But again God was merciful, and the angel of the Lord appeared to the wife of Manoah, who was of the tribe of Dan. The angel announced that her barrenness would end, and she would bear a son, who would begin to deliver Israel from the Philistines. He would be a Nazirite,[1] devoted to the Lord from his birth.

When Samson grew to manhood, he manifested the presence of the Spirit of the Lord in deeds of great physical strength. His one weakness seemed to stem from an attraction to the daughters of the Philistines. On the way to negotiate a marriage, Samson with his bare hands killed a lion that attacked him. Later when he came to claim his wife, he saw that the body of the lion had been inhabited by bees and was filled with honey. While Samson waited with 30 Philistine companions for the negotiations to be completed, he put to them a riddle based on the strange sight, promising each of them a set of clothes if they could solve it. They tried in vain to solve the riddle, and finally threatened Samson's new wife, to make her extract the answer from him. When Samson told her the answer, she repeated it to the Philistines. Samson paid his debt to them by killing 30 men of Ashkelon and giving their clothes to the 30 Philistines, and then went to his home.

---

1. A Nazirite was an Israelite who consecrated himself or herself and took a vow of separation and self-imposed abstinence for the purpose of some special service. The principal marks that distinguished the Nazirite were (1) a renunciation of wine and all products of the vine including grapes; (2) prohibition of the use of the razor; and (3) avoidance of contact with a dead body (see Numbers 6).

When Samson later went to visit his wife, he learned that she had been given away to the best man. He caught 300 foxes, tied them together in pairs by the tails with torches between, and set fire to the Philistines' fields of corn. When the Philistines, in revenge, burned Samson's wife and her father to death, Samson retaliated by killing many of them, and then went down and stayed in a cave in the rock of Etam. The Philistines demanded his return, and 3,000 men of Judah went to Samson and convinced him to allow them to deliver him bound with ropes into the Philistines' hands. When the Philistines came to take him, Samson broke the ropes and, grabbing the jawbone of a donkey, he struck down a thousand of the Philistines.

The final incident of his life centered around a third Philistine woman named Delilah. The story of her attempt to discover the secret of Samson's strength has been told around the world. Three times he gave her false answers, but when she nagged him unceasingly he finally told her the truth. Then, while he slept in her lap, she called a man to shave off all of Samson's hair. When he awoke, it is recorded that "he did not know that the Lord had left him" (Judges 16:20). Since he was unable to resist, the Philistines captured him, gouged out his eyes and put him in prison in Gaza, forcing him to grind at the prison mill. Thus God's mighty man, wretched and blinded, stands as a continuing reminder to "abstain from sinful desires, which war against your soul" (1 Peter 2:11). Left unjudged, these sinful desires will bring the mightiest saint into bondage and darkness.

But even in prison God's grace did not forsake Samson, His chosen servant. As the sightless Samson ground at the prison mill, his hair began to grow, and when the Philistine lords gathered for a great sacrifice to their god Dagon, they called Samson before them to entertain them. Samson asked the servant who led him to put him between the two great pillars that supported the temple, and praying earnestly to the Lord, he pushed the pillars apart, and the temple fell upon the rulers and the people, crushing about 3,000 men and women to death. Samson, too, died in the ruins. His life testifies that even those of great and marked spiritual ability can fall from their place of usefulness. Although God in His faithfulness will not desert them, their spiritual effectiveness is far from what it could have been.

"Everyone Did As He Saw Fit" (Judges 17-21)

The strange story of Judges 17-18 is apparently included that subsequent generations might have a picture of the ignorance and unbelief which was quickly manifested among the people of Israel when they turned from the living God. A man named Micah from the hill country of Ephraim had a shrine. He made an ephod and some idols, and installed one of his sons as his priest. The explanation is given that this was a result of the lack of central authority in the land, and so "everyone did as he saw fit" (Judges 17:6). But what they thought was "fit" was very wrong indeed. When a young Levite from Judah came by Micah's house, Micah urged him to become the family's official private priest. This he did, and became to Micah as one of his own sons.

When 600 armed men from the tribe of Dan came to the house of Micah, they enticed the young Levite to steal the ephod and the household gods, and to go with them as their official priest. Though Micah followed them to protest, he was unable to recover his lost trea-

sures, and the Danites went on to capture the city of Laish, and they renamed it Dan. There they set up their idols, and the young Levite, who turned out to be the grandson of Moses, became the head of a line of priests who served the city of Dan until the time of the Assyrian captivity. The account explains the deteriorating moral condition which later permitted Jeroboam, the son of Solomon, to set up in the city of Dan the worship of the golden calf (see 1 Kings 12).

The final story of the book of Judges, in chapters 19-21, is a flashback to the earlier days of conquest when Phinehas, grandson of Aaron, was still priest within the nation. It is one of the most sordid accounts in Scripture, and illustrates the ease with which even the most vile and repulsive sin can take root in the hearts of those who turn away from daily fellowship with the living God.

It concerns another Levite in the hill country of Ephraim whose concubine (a secondary wife) had returned to her father's home in Bethlehem. When the Levite went to bring her home, they found themselves at sunset near the Benjaminite city of Gibeah. There they sought lodging, but no one would take them in, until at last an old man, finding them abandoned in the city square, took them to his own home. That evening certain men of Benjamin who had given themselves over to homosexuality beat upon the door of the house and demanded that the stranger be brought out for their sexual indulgence. The master of the house offered them his own virgin daughter and the Levite's concubine instead. When they refused this offer, the Levite forced his concubine out the door and the men of the city took her and abused her all night.

At daybreak, the Levite opened the door and found his concubine lying dead on the threshold. He divided her body into 12 pieces and sent one to each of the tribes of Israel. This shocking deed so stunned the leaders of the people that, in response, they gathered an army of 400,000 men and marched against Benjamin. They demanded that the guilty men within the tribe be given them for punishment, but the Benjaminites refused. Instead they mustered an army of 26,000 men. The two armies met for battle before the city of Gibeah.

God allowed Benjamin to defeat the Israelites in two separate battles, killing 22,000 and then 18,000 Israelites. The double defeat may indicate that the other tribes had been corrupted by their contact with the Canaanites. The whole Israelite army went up to the house of God and fasted and wept before the Lord. This time the Lord promised to deliver the Benjaminites into their hands. A total of 25,000 Benjaminites were killed, and a remnant of 600 fled to the desert for refuge.

This terrible civil war had taken a dreadful toll, and the Israelites realized that they had virtually eliminated one of the 12 tribes. They had vowed before the Lord at Mizpah that they would not allow any of their daughters to marry Benjaminites; therefore it looked as though the tribe of Benjamin was doomed to extinction. Realizing what a breach this would make in their nation, they settled on a terrible remedy. Learning that the city of Jabesh in Gilead had not sent any armed men to the conflict, they killed every male and every married woman in the city. They brought back 400 young virgins, and these they offered to the remaining 600 men of Benjamin for wives. They encouraged the remaining 200 men of Benjamin to lie in wait at the city of Shiloh, and when the young women of the city came out to celebrate one of the annual festivals, they were to fall upon them and take them for wives.

The book closes with the reminder that these things were the result of "everyone [doing] as he saw fit" (Judges 21:25). The terrible record of Judges is one of vile idolatry, treachery, betrayals, civil war and ruthless human connivance. It should be read frequently as a reminder of the fatal weakness which can permit the blackest of sins to take root when the heart no longer fellowships daily with God.

Ruth

The Book of Ruth opens with the story of a man named Elimelech, who with his wife Naomi and their two sons left Bethlehem because of a famine and went to live in the country of Moab. The story takes place in the days of the judges, and it is instructive to note that in Bethlehem ("the house of food") there was no food, but a famine. The book of Leviticus has already told us that famine indicates a low level of spiritual vitality within the affected nation. In Moab, Elimelech died and his two sons, Mahlon and Kilion, married women of Moab, Orpah and Ruth. After 10 years the two sons also died, and Naomi was left with her two daughters-in-law.

On expressing her determination to return to Bethlehem, having learned that the famine was over, Naomi exhorted her daughters-in-law to remain in Moab and remarry there. Orpah was unwilling to leave her home for an uncertain life in Israel, but Ruth refused to stay in Moab, and, in a plea of enduring beauty, declared her determination to identify herself with Naomi's land and people. The deepest cause of her determination is seen in her statement in Ruth 1:16, "Your God [will be] my God." This clearly represents her willingness to leave the idols of Moab for the worship of the living God of Israel.

So the two arrived in Bethlehem at the beginning of the barley harvest with a very uncertain future before them. The invisible hand of the Lord in caring for His own is apparent in the statement that Ruth went into the fields to glean, and, "as it turned out, she found herself working in a field belonging to Boaz" (Ruth 2:3). This man, a close relative of Elimelech, Naomi's husband, appears in the story as a man of unusual character and sensitivity. He had heard the full story of Naomi and Ruth's return to Bethlehem. Upon meeting Ruth in his fields, he commended her for her kindness to her mother-in-law, and especially for her faith in the God of Israel, under whose gracious wings she had taken refuge.

Obviously attracted to the beautiful Moabite woman, and yet acting always with restraint and dignity, Boaz instructed his workmen to deliberately leave grain in the field for Ruth to glean. When she returned to Naomi in the evening with an unexpected abundance, she learned for the first time from her mother-in-law that Boaz was a possible kinsman-redeemer.[1] At Naomi's instruction, she continued gleaning in Boaz's fields through the barley and wheat harvests.

At the end of the harvest, when the winnowing of the barley took place, Naomi seized the initiative provided by her relationship with Boaz and instructed Ruth on a strategy that would combine both the law of redemption and the law of Levirate marriage.[2] By coming to the sleeping Boaz and lying at his feet, Ruth followed a custom in Israel by which she was essentially asking Boaz to fulfill the responsibility of a kinsman to marry her and raise up heirs to the deceased Elimelech. She did this so modestly that Boaz commended her for her action, and having now clearly fallen in love with her, he eagerly consented to take on the requested responsibility. He had evidently hoped that such a situation would occur, for he immediately informed Ruth that a closer kinsman was involved and his claim must be settled first. In the morning he sent her back to Naomi with a gift of six measures of barley, and Naomi reassured her that the matter would surely be settled that day.

That same morning, Boaz took his seat at the gate of the town, where the elders gathered for the judging of matters brought before them. When the closer kinsman came by, Boaz presented his case to him. He declared that Naomi wanted to sell a piece of land which belonged to Elimelech, but if she did the next of kin would be responsible to care for the family. Seeing the possibility of obtaining a choice piece of property, the first kinsman declared his willingness to assume this responsibility, but then Boaz played his trump card. He informed him that the land was also encumbered by a Levirate marriage, and that if he bought the property he would also have to marry the woman. This changed the picture for the first kinsman, since the land would then belong not to him but to whatever issue resulted from his union with Ruth. The man removed his right sandal and handed it to Boaz in the presence of the witnesses. The sandal symbolized his right as owner to set foot upon the land. This right now became Boaz's and the coast was clear for him to take Ruth as his wife.

The account closes with the birth to Boaz and Ruth of a son, who brought great joy to the heart of his grandmother, Naomi, and grew up to be the grandfather of David, Israel's mightiest king.

The beautiful story of Ruth not only provides a link between the days of the judges and the subsequent reign of David, but symbolizes in the figure of Boaz how Christ our great Kinsman-Redeemer overcomes the obstacle of our birth in Adam, as strangers and foreigners to the promises of God, and takes us to Himself in a union that will produce the fruit of the Spirit to the honor and glory of God.

It is significant that in the genealogy of Matthew, Ruth is included as the ancestress of Jesus the Messiah. As surely as the book of Judges reveals the depravity into which the Israelites had fallen, and the wickedness humanity is capable of when everyone does what he or she sees fit, so the book of Ruth, which is set during that time, reminds us that no matter how evil the time, God has His people; no matter how hopeless a situation may seem, God is greater (see Romans 5:20; 11:4-5). No matter what, God's plan and purpose will be accomplished (see Psalm 33:11).

---

1. A kinsman-redeemer was a male relative who, according to various laws found in the Pentateuch, had the privilege or responsibility to act for a relative who was in trouble, danger, or need of vindication. (Baker's Evangelical Dictionary of Biblical Theology)

2. According to God's law, if a widow had no sons, the brother or close relative of the deceased husband was to marry the widow. The first son of their union would be counted as the deceased husband's son and would inherit his estate. (See Deuteronomy 25:5-6.)

Study Questions

Before you begin your study this week:

- ֍ Pray and ask God to speak to you through His Holy Spirit.
- ֍ Use only the Bible for your answers.
- ֍ Write down your answers and the verses you used.
- ֍ Answer the "Challenge" questions if you have the time and want to do them.
- ֍ Share your answers to the "Personal" questions with the class only if you want to share them.

First Day: Read the Commentary on Judges & Ruth.

1. What meaningful or new thought did you find in the Commentary on Judges and Ruth, or from your teacher's lecture? What personal application did you choose to apply to your life?

2. Look for a verse in the lesson to memorize this week. Write it down, carry it with you, tack it to your bulletin board, on the dashboard of your car, etc. Make a real effort to learn the verse and its "address" (reference of where it is found in the Bible).

3. This week's questions focus on the book of 1 Samuel. If you have time, you may want to read through the entire book this week. As you answer the questions, you will be looking up passages of Scripture from various places in the Bible. This will help you discover that God's Word is a "whole," and that His message to us is the same from Genesis to Revelation.

First and Second Samuel were originally one book. First Samuel forms a link between the decadence of the period of the judges and the rise of the monarchy. It is the story of three men—Samuel, the last of the judges and the first of the prophets; Saul, the first king of Israel; and David, the greatest of all of Israel's kings.

Second Day:

The book of 1 Samuel opens as the dark and turbulent time of the judges was nearing its end. The Philistines were still oppressing Israel. The tabernacle was located at Shiloh, with Eli and his sons serving as priests.

1. a. In 1 Samuel 1 we are introduced to Hannah. Describe Hannah's prayer and her vow in verses 10-11.

   b. What was the outcome of her prayer? (verse 20)

   c. How did Hannah fulfill her vow? (verses 24-28)

2. Challenge: First Samuel 2:1-10 is Hannah's prayer of thanksgiving and praise. What are some of the Lord's characteristics and deeds that she extols?

3. Visions from the Lord were rare in those days, yet the word of the Lord came to the boy Samuel. What do you learn about Samuel from 1 Samuel 3:19—4:1a?

4. a. After Samuel reached adulthood, there came a time when the people of Israel mourned and sought after the Lord. Read 1 Samuel 7:3-6. What step were the Israelites to take if they were truly returning to the Lord? (verses 3-4)

    b. What did Israel do at Mizpah? (verses 5-6)

5. a. Read 1 Samuel 7:7-11. What did the Philistines do when they learned that the Israelites had assembled at Mizpah? (verse 7a)

    b. What transpired after that? (verses 7b-11, summarize briefly)

6. a. What action did Samuel take in 1 Samuel 7:12?

    b. Personal: Sometimes when a person turns to the Lord in repentance, the enemy of our souls will attempt to discourage them from walking with the Lord. But if they continue to seek the Lord, He will give them victory. Have you or someone you know experienced this? If so, what happened?

Third Day:

1. Read 1 Samuel 7:15-17, and summarize Samuel's judgeship.

2. Read 1 Samuel 8:4-5. When Samuel was old, what did the elders of Israel ask for, and what two reasons did they give for this request?

3. What did God say regarding this? (1 Samuel 8:7-9)

4. Read 1 Samuel 10:1 and 11:15. Whom did Samuel anoint and the people confirm as leader of God's inheritance?

5. Personal: The Israelites wanted a king like "all the other nations have" (1 Samuel 8:5). Their excuse was the behavior of Samuel's sons. Many Scripture verses, including Romans 12:2, tell us that we are not to be like the world, and yet we justify our attitudes and actions, trying to separate our daily lives from the Lord and His ways. Can you think of some ways people do this today, such as saying, "That's just business," when they do something not ethical or morally right in their business dealings?

Fourth Day:

1. In 1 Samuel 13, the Philistines again assembled a large army to fight against Israel. This so frightened the Israelite men that they scattered and hid. At Samuel's instruction, Saul and a small band of men waited for Samuel to come to make an offering prior to battle. When the prophet delayed, Saul took on himself the priestly office and made the sacrifice.[1] From 1 Samuel 13:10-14, what was the result of this?

2. God gave Saul one last chance to redeem himself as king. He commanded Saul, through Samuel, to launch an attack on the Amalekites and to utterly destroy them and everything they owned, including their livestock. From 1 Samuel 15:7-9, was Saul victorious in battle? How obedient was he to God's instructions?

3. From 1 Samuel 15:20-21, how did Saul respond when Samuel confronted him about this?

4. What did God have to say regarding Saul's actions? (1 Samuel 15:22-23)

5. Personal: Saul was rejected as king and lost all that he could have had, all that he could have accomplished, because of his disobedience. Is there some area of your life in which you are living in disobedience to the Lord? Will you make the choice to repent and obey Him?

Fifth Day:

David was a "man after [God's] own heart" (1 Samuel 13:14; Acts 13:22). His story begins when God sent Samuel to the home of Jesse in Bethlehem to choose a new king from among Jesse's eight sons.

1. Read 1 Samuel 16:7. How was God's choice made?

2. What happened when David was anointed? (1 Samuel 16:13-14)

3. a. How was David first introduced into Saul's court? (1 Samuel 16:16-18)

   b. What would happen when David played his harp? (1 Samuel 16:23)

4. David became a member of Saul's army when he defeated Goliath the Philistine giant (1 Samuel 17). He was eventually promoted to high command, became close friends with Saul's son Jonathan, married Saul's daughter Michal, and became a favorite of the people. From the following verses, how did Saul feel about David, and what did Saul do because of this?

   1 Samuel 18:6-12, summarize briefly

---

1. Only priests were allowed to offer sacrifices.

1 Samuel 18:28-29

1 Samuel 19:9-11

5. Saul envied David and was fearful that David would take his throne. What does James 3:16 tell us about envy and selfish ambition?

6. Personal: Most everyone has struggled with envy at one time or another. Do you currently have envy in your heart, perhaps of someone's accomplishments, talents, possessions, or even God-given gifts? If so, go to the Lord, ask His forgiveness, and ask Him to help you be content with the blessings He has given to you.

Sixth Day:

1. a. Finally, in order to save his life, David fled from Saul. David first sought refuge with the Philistines of Gath. When that didn't work, where did he go? (1 Samuel 22:1a)

    b. Who joined him there?

2. What did David seek and receive from the king of Moab? (1 Samuel 22:3-4)

3. Personal: Until the end of his life, Saul continued unceasing persecution of David. It was during this time that David wrote many of the psalms, which speak of God's faithfulness. Do you have a favorite psalm? What is particularly meaningful to you about this psalm?

4. When given the opportunity to kill Saul, what did David say? (1 Samuel 26:9-11a)

5. Three of Saul's sons were killed in battle with the Philistines. How did Saul's life end? (1 Samuel 31:1-4)

6. Personal: David could have become discouraged or bitter because of Saul's persecution; however, he chose to trust the Lord. Are you experiencing persecution or having a difficult time with someone? Instead of taking matters into your own hands, will you trust the situation to the Lord? Write John 16:33, and personalize it by inserting your own name.

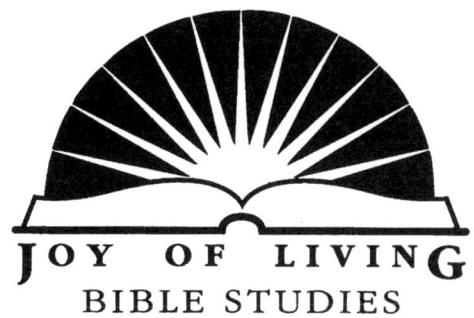

1 Samuel — The Sinful Nature and the Spirit[1]

First Samuel forms a link between the decadence of the period of the judges and the rise of the monarchy—first Saul and then David. It is the story of three men—Samuel, the last of the judges and the first of the prophets; Saul, the first king of Israel; and David, the greatest of all of Israel's kings. In the contrasting lives of Saul and David, we will see the eternal conflict between the proud heart, which finds confidence in itself, and the humble spirit, which looks to God in utter dependence and thus receives all the fullness of His blessing.

Samuel: Voice of God (1 Samuel 1-7)

In 1 Samuel we meet another of the great women of the Old Testament. Like Sarah and Rachel, Hannah was barren. Though her husband Elkanah loved her, Hannah's life was made miserable by Elkanah's second wife, Peninnah, who taunted Hannah because of her barrenness, while boasting of her own fertility.

Hannah's barrenness illustrates the spiritual barrenness of Israel. The priesthood, which God had set up with the tabernacle as a means by which the people would have access to Him, had degenerated to mere ritual and ceremony, and was no longer a potent factor in maintaining the vitality of faith within the nation.

Hannah, however, was a woman of quiet faith. In great distress, she took her problem of barrenness to the Lord at the tabernacle in Shiloh. As she prayed, Eli the priest saw her lips move but heard no sound, so he thought she was drunk. When Eli rebuked her, Hannah explained that she had been promising God that if He would give her a son she would dedicate him to the service of the Lord all his life. Eli pronounced a blessing on her, and she and her husband returned to their home. In due course, the promised son was given, and Hannah named him Samuel. True to her vow, when the child was weaned, around three years of age or older,[2] Hannah brought him to the tabernacle and left him in the care of Eli to serve the Lord.

The state of spiritual decay in the priesthood was clearly visible in the lives of Eli's two sons. He only mildly rebuked their evil conduct, and in due course the Lord sent an unnamed man of God to Eli to announce that the priesthood would eventually be taken away from

his descendants. This prophecy was fulfilled in the days of Solomon. The promise of "a faithful priest, who will do according to what is in my heart and mind" (1 Samuel 2:35), seems to anticipate the coming of the Messiah and the eternal priesthood of the Lord Jesus.

The account of the boy Samuel being called by the direct voice of the Lord is reminiscent of the appearing of God to Moses in the desert of Midian. The nature of Samuel's ministry as an authentic prophet of the Lord was indicated by God's revelation to him of the fate of Eli and his sons. As Samuel grew to manhood, he became widely recognized as God's prophet, so that "all Israel from Dan to Beersheba recognized that Samuel was attested as a prophet of the LORD" (1 Samuel 3:20).

After a military defeat at the hands of the Philistines, the Israelites, instead of seeking God, superstitiously demanded that the Ark of the Covenant be taken from the tabernacle and accompany them in battle. Total disaster followed. Thousands of Israelites were killed, including the two sons of Eli, and the Philistines captured the ark. When news of his sons' death was brought to Eli, he fell over and died. When his pregnant daughter-in-law heard, she went into labor and gave birth to a son. In view of the terrible circumstances, she named the child Ichabod ("the glory has departed").

Though the presence of the Ark of the Covenant in battle did not bring victory to Israel, the Philistines found it to be a source of torment. The ark was placed in the temple of Dagon, the Philistine god. On two successive mornings the Philistines found their idol toppled. Next a plague of tumors broke out among the people of the city of Ashdod, who hastily sent the ark to Gath. There the tumors broke out again.

Finally, in desperation, the rulers of the Philistines decided to return the ark to Israel, along with an offering to the God of Israel. In order to determine whether Israel's God was actually behind the plague, the Philistines hitched two milk cows to a cart, but shut up the cows' calves at home. Contrary to nature, the cows drew the cart away from their calves and directly to Beth Shemesh, which was the first city within the border of Israel.

Here God taught the people a lesson in reverence, for when, contrary to the law, 70 men of Beth Shemesh looked into the ark out of curiosity, they immediately died. Frightened by this slaughter, the inhabitants of Beth Shemesh sent the ark to Kiriath Jearim. There it was put into the care of Eleazar, a Levite, and it remained for 20 years.

Samuel seized the occasion of Israel's renewed fear of the Lord to urge the people to put away their idols and to serve the Lord only.

1. This is an overview. You can study 1 Samuel in more detail in the Joy of Living study titled *1 Samuel*.
2. It was customary in the East to nurse children three years or longer. (*The NIV Study Bible*. See note on 1 Samuel 1:22.)

The people gathered at Mizpah and confessed their sin. As Samuel was sacrificing the burnt offering, the Philistines attacked, but they were routed by a mighty thundering from the Lord. The subsequent great victory over the Philistines was memorialized by a stone, which Samuel erected and named Ebenezer, "the stone of help."

Saul: Man of Sinful Nature (1 Samuel 8-15)

Saul, the first king of Israel, was a young man of handsome physique and apparently modest disposition. He nevertheless proved to have little real concern for the things of God. He began his career with bright promise. But a shadow over his reign was seen from the very beginning, when the people demanded a king "like all the other nations" (1 Samuel 8:20). This was a denial of Israel's very purpose, for they had been called to be *unlike* all the other nations, and were to be a people directly governed by God.[1] But, as so many times before, God permitted them to have their way, that they might learn from the sad results the nature of their folly. The principle of the sinful nature is thus seen at work in the nation of Israel, destroying its communion and enjoyment of God's blessing. The same principle is interwoven in every Christian life. The desire of the sinful nature is to be religious in a manner acceptable to the world, and to conduct its business by the principles of the world.

As Saul's story begins, his father's donkeys had strayed off, and Saul was sent in search of them. After a long and fruitless search he providentially ended up at the town where Samuel lived. Saul's servant suggested that they consult the prophet as to the location of the donkeys. So Saul went to Samuel, and to his amazement he found that Samuel was expecting him, for God had told Samuel that a young man from Benjamin would appear the next day, and Samuel was to anoint him as king over Israel. Samuel privately anointed Saul as the new king. In due course the people were called together at Mizpah for the formal presentation of their new king. As Saul stood among the people, they raised a great shout, for he looked the very picture of a king, towering head and shoulders above everyone.

The first test of his kingship came with an attack by the Ammonites. Stirred by the Spirit of God, Saul sent word to the 12 tribes to gather an army, and 330,000 men responded. A great victory resulted, and in the midst of it Saul manifested a spirit of fairness and mercy toward some who had refused to acknowledge his kingship.

Responding to Samuel's call, the people gathered at Gilgal and there renewed their vows to the Lord. Samuel delivered a farewell address, for though he would continue to serve as prophet, it would be in a somewhat more private manner. He reminded Israel that deliverance had always come to them when they walked in obedience to God, but disaster had befallen them whenever they turned from Him. Now even though their insistence on having a king meant a partial rejection of the government of God, the old prophet promised them that the Lord would not cast away His people for His own name's sake, and he, Samuel, would continue to pray for them and teach them.

1. Though in Deuteronomy provision had been made for a king, he was to be a man of humble spirit and obedient heart, who would be the human instrument of the government of God.

Chapters 13 and 14 are a summary of Saul's wars with the Philistines. Saul first amassed a standing army of 3,000 men and put part of it under his son, Jonathan, who attacked the Philistine outpost at Geba. This brought on a massive mustering of the Philistine army, which so frightened the Israelites that they fled before them and hid.

Meanwhile, Saul waited at Gilgal with his small army for Samuel to come and make offerings for their success. When the prophet delayed beyond the seven appointed days, Saul took on himself the priestly office and, as he explained to Samuel when he came, "I felt compelled to offer the burnt offering" (1 Samuel 13:12). Samuel rebuked this self-dependent spirit with the announcement that, because of Saul's act, his kingdom would be taken away and given to another man.

While the people trembled before the oncoming Philistines, Jonathan and his armor-bearer manifested great confidence in the power of God to act on their behalf. The two men made a remarkable attack on the foe, resulting in the killing of 20 men. This unexpected attack produced panic among the Philistines, and seeing it, the Israelites emerged from hiding to complete the rout of the Philistines.

God gave Saul one last chance to redeem himself as king. He commanded Saul, through Samuel, to launch an attack on the Amalekites and utterly destroy them. Saul's campaign was victorious, but again he proved disobedient, for he spared King Agag of the Amalekites and also saved the best of the livestock. His sinful nature is thus revealed, for he presumed to find something good in what God had declared utterly bad. This is a clear picture of what many Christians do today when they refuse to judge the manifestations of the sinful nature, but excuse them as part of their personality or temperament.

When Samuel came to Saul, having been told of Saul's disobedience by the Lord, Saul told him that he had completely performed the commandment of the Lord. However Saul's self-commendatory speech was interrupted by the telltale bleating of the sheep and lowing of the cattle which he had spared. Saul lamely excused himself as having saved them for sacrificial purposes, but Samuel bluntly interrupted his hypocrisy with the announcement that the Lord had rejected him from being king over Israel. In the course of his rebuke he reminded Saul that obedience is the first and greatest service to God. Samuel called for a sword and himself killed the Amalekite king. Then Samuel returned to his home, never to see Saul again. However, he grieved over the disobedient king.

King Saul is symbolic of the person who lives according to the sinful nature, for in him we see the ruin which is caused by the mind which is set on what that nature desires. By contrast, David, introduced in chapter 16, is a beautiful illustration of the mind which is set on what the Spirit desires (see Romans 8:5-6).

David: Man of Faith (1 Samuel 16-31)

The story of David is the story of a "man after [God's] own heart" (1 Samuel 13:14; Acts 13:22). David's story begins when God sent Samuel to the home of Jesse in Bethlehem to choose a king from among Jesse's eight sons. When the seven older sons passed before Samuel, each one looked like a king in the making, but God said to

Samuel of each, "This is not the one that I have chosen." At last David was brought in from the fields, where he had been watching his father's sheep. Though David was handsome, the choice was not made by outward appearance, for God declared that He looked at the heart. At David's anointing, the Spirit of God came upon him in power, and remained with him throughout his life.

In the meantime the Spirit of the Lord had departed from Saul, and we are told, "An evil spirit from the LORD tormented him" (1 Samuel 16:14). God allowed evil spirits to have access to Saul's mind and heart, since Saul had chosen to reject the ways and resources of God. As the apostle Paul warns us, to give way to the desires of the sinful nature is to give the devil a foothold (see Ephesians 4:17-27). The result in Saul's life was that he experienced attacks of mental disturbance, expressed in violent outbursts of rage. To calm him in these times a skilled musician was recommended, and in the providence of God, David was brought to play his harp in the king's court.

David was not to be set on the throne immediately, as Saul had been, but was tested and proved by struggle and adversity. This is the principle God often follows with the person who learns to walk by faith. We are put through a time of obscurity and adversity. Everything seems to go against us, until at last we recognize the principle by which God's activity is always enacted—we can do nothing in ourselves, but only in complete dependence upon the God who indwells us.

At this time the armies of Israel were being taunted by the giant Goliath, who paraded up and down, mocking the impotence of the Israelites who did not dare to send a man into combat against him. When David came from his flock to bring food to his brothers in the army, he found the whole camp of Israel plunged into despair. While he was there, the giant came again. David's question to the men standing near him was, "Who is this uncircumcised Philistine that he should defy the armies of the living God?" (1 Samuel 17:26). That is always the outlook of faith. It is not shaken by circumstances, but looks beyond them to the God who is greater than all circumstances.

Word was brought to Saul of the young man who was contemptuous of the challenge of the Philistine giant. When Saul saw how young David was, he attempted to dismiss him, but David reassured him with stories of how he had killed both bears and lions when they attacked his father's sheep. Saul consented to David fighting the giant and, in an effort to be helpful, put his own armor on David. But David found it impossible to use the armor. Instead he went down to the stream and chose five smooth stones for his sling.

When the Philistine champion saw David coming, he cursed David for his youth and vowed to give his flesh to the birds of the air and the beasts of the field, but David calmly replied, "This day the LORD will hand you over to me" (1 Samuel 17:46). David's faith rested in the assurance that "the battle is the LORD's" (1 Samuel 17:47). Hurling a stone from his sling, he struck the giant between the eyes, and Goliath fell face down on the ground. David ran and seized the giant's own sword and cut off his head with it.

Because of his great victory over Goliath, David had now become the sensation of the nation, and Saul eyed him with increasing envy

from that day on. Twice, in his madness, Saul tried to kill David with his spear, but both times David evaded him. In sharp contrast with this, Saul's son Jonathan openly sought friendship with David, and it is recorded that he "loved him as himself" (1 Samuel 18:1).[1]

Saul again attempted to kill David, and once again David escaped. The king then sent soldiers to David's house to take him, but Michal, David's wife, let him down through a window and reported to the messengers that David was ill. When her duplicity was discovered, she excused it to her father, Saul, by claiming David had threatened to kill her if she did not aid his escape.

David fled to Samuel at Ramah. When Saul sent messengers after him, he was protected by direct divine intervention, in which the Spirit of God turned back three companies of soldiers by compelling them to prophesy. At last when Saul himself came to capture David, he too was seized by the Spirit of God and prophesied before Samuel.

From here to the end of the book, we find the story of the unceasing persecution of David by Saul, illustrating the principle Paul declares in Galatians 4:29, "The son born in the ordinary way persecuted the son born by the power of the Spirit." It was during these days of constant flight that David wrote many of the psalms, which speak of God's faithfulness in distressing conditions.

Through the painful persecution that David experienced, God was preparing him for the work that lay before him. He fled to Nob, the city of priests. There, needing bread, he was given the bread of the Presence from the table in the tabernacle. Centuries later, Jesus would refer to this incident and justify David's conduct as the actions of a man of faith (see Matthew 12).

However, the next incident reveals David's occasional fear, for he sought refuge among the Philistines in the city of Gath. There he found his reputation as a valiant warrior had preceded him. To avoid being killed by the Philistines, he pretended to be mad, letting his saliva run down his beard. It is sad to see the anointed of the Lord reduced to such tactics to save his own skin. The story stands as a warning against taking refuge among those who are the Lord's enemies.

When Saul was told by Doeg the Edomite about David's visit to Ahimelech the priest, Saul summoned the entire body of priests to his presence. There he accused them of harboring David and ordered them to be killed. When the king's soldiers refused to kill the Lord's priests, Doeg himself killed 85 priests. Abiathar, one of the sons of Ahimelech, escaped the slaughter and joined David in his hiding place.

King Saul's relentless pursuit of David meant that the affairs of the kingdom were falling into disarray. The Philistines took full advantage of this, and attacked the city of Keilah. It was David, rather than Saul, who responded. With 600 of the men who had joined him, he overcame the Philistines and saved the city. When David learned that Saul had heard he was in Keilah and was sending an army against

1. Jonathan was a godly man; David was a man after God's own heart (see Acts 13:22); and the friendship between them was God's gift to them both. Some might say the friendship God blessed them with was an ungodly relationship; however, homosexuality is detestable to the Lord (see Leviticus 20:13). That being said, there can be deep friendships, deep love, between people without sex or sexual attraction being involved.

him, David consulted the Lord through his priest, Abiathar, and learned that the men of the city were ready to give him up to Saul's vengeance.

Again he fled, this time to the Desert of Ziph. There Jonathan sought him out and encouraged his heart with reminders that God had determined to make him king over Israel. The Ziphites attempted to betray David to Saul, but David was spared when the Philistines launched another attack, and Saul had to turn aside from his pursuit.

David's greatness of spirit is revealed by the account of Saul's renewed pursuit of him after returning from the battle with the Philistines. Saul unwittingly entered the very cave in which David and his men were hiding. While Saul was in there, David managed to cut off a corner of Saul's robe. After Saul left the cave, David came out and held up the piece of robe as proof that when he had Saul in his power he did not take vengeance, but rather honored him as the Lord's anointed and spared his life. Saul seemed to be moved by this mercy on David's part, and acknowledged that David would indeed be king some day. But David and his men returned to their stronghold.

The death of Samuel in 1 Samuel 25 meant that Israel had lost a great voice for God and a great prayer warrior for the people. We then find the account of Nabal (which means "fool") and his wife, Abigail. When this wealthy farmer was shearing his sheep in Carmel, David sent ten of his young men to ask for a supply of food, reminding Nabal that the safety he enjoyed was due to the presence of David and his men. Nabal churlishly refused, and David, angered, gathered his men to wreak vengeance upon the foolish man.

When Nabal's wife Abigail heard that David was intent upon their destruction, she hastily sent David a generous present of food. Mounting her donkey, she met David on his way to take revenge. There, with gracious words she reasoned with him, reminding him that he was taking vengeance into his own hands and this would be evil in the eyes of the Lord. David commended her for the service she had rendered him in preventing a bloody deed on his part. The next morning, when Abigail told her husband Nabal of his narrow escape from death, the shock brought on an attack, which ten days later resulted in his death.

When David heard of Nabal's death, he sent his servants and asked Abigail to be his wife. We are told that David had also married Ahinoam of Jezreel, in place of his former wife Michal, whom Saul had given to another. Here we have evidence of a weakness in David which would ultimately lead him into the most terrible sin of his life.

Once again Saul pursued David with an army of 3,000 men. One night David and two of his men stole into Saul's camp amidst the sleeping men. David took Saul's spear and water jug and left the camp. Then, standing some distance away, he called out, waking the king and his men. David again reminded Saul that he had had an opportunity to take his life, but spared him because Saul was the Lord's anointed. Once again Saul was moved with remorse and confessed to David, "I have acted like a fool" (1 Samuel 26:21). But he made no attempt to restore David to his rightful place, and the account ends with Saul returning to his headquarters and David again going into exile.

David now sought refuge among the Philistines, this time with all his men, and King Achish gave him the town of Ziklag. From there David carried out raids against other Canaanite enemies of Israel. David deceived Achish into thinking his attacks were directed against the cities of Israel. It is clear that when a believer takes refuge among those who are the enemies of faith, he or she is in great danger of violating some fundamental principle of righteousness himself. Surely the God who had delivered David from Goliath could also have kept him from Saul, without the necessity of taking refuge among the Philistines. This dallying with the Philistines resulted in David being compelled to join the Philistine army in preparing to launch an attack upon Israel.

When King Saul learned that the Philistines were gathering against him, he was afraid and sought the Lord for guidance, but the Lord refused to answer him in any manner. In desperation, Saul disguised himself and sought out a medium, though God had forbidden it, and he himself had given orders, long before, that all mediums should be put to death. Saul asked the medium of Endor to call Samuel from the dead to advise Saul. The Bible doesn't tell us whether God sent an impersonating spirit as the medium expected, or sent the true spirit of Samuel, but Saul believed it was Samuel, who announced Saul's impending death on the battlefield the next day.

When the rulers of the Philistines saw David among them, they protested to King Achish and forced David to turn back. When David returned to Ziklag he found that the Amalekites had sacked the city. He sought the guidance of God and set out in pursuit. He managed to overtake and destroy the raiders, recovering his two wives and great quantities of spoil. He insisted that 200 of his men who had been too exhausted to join him should share equally in the spoil with those who had gone with him, for he maintained that it was the Lord who had delivered the enemy into his hands, and not those who fought.

While David was being delivered from his enemies, Saul and the Israelite army where not having the same success. As the Israelites fled before the Philistines, Saul's three sons were killed. Although Saul was a mighty warrior, the fighting was fierce, and archers critically wounded him. Fearing that the Philistines would capture and torture him, Saul asked his armor bearer to kill him, but he refused. In desperation, Saul fell on his own sword, killing himself. When the armor bearer saw that Saul was dead, he too fell on his sword.

Saul joined Samuel in the life beyond, but as one whose earthly life was essentially wasted, and whose opportunity for service in eternity was thereby diminished. What a tragic end for Saul. From the time he was publicly acknowledged as king until the day of his death, Saul had difficulty obeying the Lord. Even at the end, he took matters into his own hands rather than trusting the Lord. How different his life would have been if he had consistently sought to obey the Lord.

What about you? Do you look back on your life with peace, knowing that you have tried to walk in obedience to the Lord, however imperfectly—or do you wonder how different it might have been if you had not lived in rebellion against Him? If the latter is the case, remember, you are still alive; you still have the opportunity to repent and choose to use your remaining time walking in His ways. Won't you make that choice now?

Study Questions

Before you begin your study this week:

- ❧ Pray and ask God to speak to you through His Holy Spirit.
- ❧ Use only the Bible for your answers.
- ❧ Write down your answers and the verses you used.
- ❧ Answer the "Challenge" questions if you have the time and want to do them.
- ❧ Share your answers to the "Personal" questions with the class only if you want to share them.

First Day: Read the Commentary on 1 Samuel.

1. What meaningful or new thought did you find in the Commentary on 1 Samuel, or from your teacher's lecture? What personal application did you choose to apply to your life?

2. Look for a verse in the lesson to memorize this week. Write it down, carry it with you, tack it to your bulletin board, on the dashboard of your car, etc. Make a real effort to learn the verse and its "address" (reference of where it is found in the Bible).

3. This week's questions focus on the books of 2 Samuel and 1 Chronicles. If you have time, you may want to read through both books this week. As you answer the questions, you will be looking up passages of Scripture from various places in the Bible. This will help you discover that God's Word is a "whole," and that His message to us is the same from Genesis to Revelation.

The books of 2 Samuel and 1 Chronicles cover the same period of time, although from quite distinct viewpoints. Although they do not follow one another in the biblical order, they may be studied as one book. They both center upon the story of one man—David, the king "after [God's] own heart" (1 Samuel 13:14; Acts 13:22).

Second Day:

1. a. Second Samuel opens with a second account of the death of Saul, and a lament expressing David's grief. Read 2 Samuel 2:1-4a. What did David ask God, and what answer did he receive? (verse 1)

   b. What did the men of Judah do? (verse 4a)

2. a. Although David's own tribe, Judah, anointed him king, there were eleven other tribes of Israel. What took place with them after Saul's death? (2 Samuel 2:8-9)

   b. From 2 Samuel 3:1, describe the conflict between the house of Saul and the house of David.

3. The conflict ended when two men murdered Ishbosheth and brought his head to David, thinking to gain his approval. Instead of giving them a reward, David had them put to death. From 2 Samuel 5:1-3, what did the tribes of Israel do after the death of Ishbosheth?

4. How old was David when He became king over all of Israel? (2 Samuel 5:4)

5. Personal: David waited many years for God to fulfill His promises. Perhaps you are wondering when, or even if, God will fulfill His promises to you. What does Hebrews 10:35-36 say to you about this?

Third Day:

David's first act as king over a united Israel was to capture the city of Jerusalem and make it his capital. Following this, he built a magnificent palace of cedar in Jerusalem.

1. From 2 Samuel 5:10, why did David become more and more powerful?

2. a. Read 2 Samuel 5:17-19, 25. How did the Philistines react when they learned that David was king over Israel? (verse 17a)

    b. What action did David take? (verses 17b-19, 25a)

    c. What was the result of David's obedience to the Lord? (verse 25b)

3. What does 1 Chronicles 14:17 say regarding the nations around Israel?

4. David planned to centralize the worship of the Lord, and he prepared a place for the ark in Jerusalem. However, the first time he attempted to move the ark ended disastrously with the death of one of his men. From 1 Chronicles 15:12-15, why did this happen, and what should David have done differently?

5. From 1 Chronicles 16:1-4, summarize the celebration that took place when David brought the ark into the tabernacle.

6. Personal: It was with great joy that the ark was placed within the tabernacle in Jerusalem, but it was also with a renewed fear of the Lord. Like David, we must learn that in serving God, sincerity is never enough, for we can be sincerely wrong. It is not God's responsibility to carry out our program; it is rather our responsibility to be in such a relationship to Him that He may carry out His program through us. Have you ever been—or are you now—busy with your own projects for the Lord, but have failed to ask God if this is what He wants you to do, or if this the way He wants you to do it?

Fourth Day:

David was settled in his palace, and the Lord had given him rest from his enemies.

1. In 2 Samuel 7:1-2, what did David say to Nathan the prophet?

2. Summarize God's response to this from 2 Samuel 7:5-16.

3. Summarize David's response to God from 2 Samuel 7:18-29.

4. Personal: Do you stand in awe of God—of all He has done for you in the past, and of all He has promised to do for you in the future? Write a paragraph or a psalm of thanksgiving to the Lord for all these things.

Fifth Day:

The next part of the story of David tells of his tragic downfall, and of the entrance of sudden and terrible sin into his life.

1. "In the spring, at the time when kings go off to war" (2 Samuel 11:1), for some unknown reason David sent out his army but he himself stayed home in Jerusalem. Summarize what happened in 2 Samuel 11:2-5.

2. How did David attempt to cover up this sin? (2 Samuel 11:6-13; summarize briefly)

3. When this plan failed, what plan did David implement? (2 Samuel 11:14-17)

4. With Uriah out of the way, what did David do? How did the Lord feel about all of this? (2 Samuel 11:26-27)

5. When God, through Nathan the prophet, confronted David with his sin, David confessed his guilt and was forgiven. However, there were still consequences that he and his descendants would face. From 2 Samuel 12:10-14, list those consequences.

6. Personal: In all of this David accepted God's judgment without complaint, and was grateful for His mercy. David wrote Psalm 51 after this. Are you struggling with the guilt of some sin, perhaps something you did long ago, yet you just can't seem to get past it? You may want to make Psalm 51 your personal prayer. If you believe God's Word is true, personalize 1 John 1:9 by inserting your name.

Sixth Day:

The consequences of David's sin were far reaching. Bathsheba's son died; David's son Amnon committed incest with his half-sister, Tamar; in revenge, Tamar's full brother, Absalom, killed Amnon, then fled for his life. Absalom later tried to overthrow David's throne, and slept with a number of David's concubines in a tent in full view of the people of Jerusalem. He was eventually killed in battle.

1. For his own purpose, David took a census of the fighting men of Israel. God's judgment was three days of plague throughout the land. Desiring to show mercy, what did God instruct David to do, and what was the result? (2 Samuel 24:18, 19, 25)

2. a. Read 1 Chronicles 22:1-6. David is referring to the threshing floor of Araunah. What does he say in verse 1 regarding this area?

    b. What did David do in preparation for this, and why? (verses 2-5)

    c. What did David charge Solomon to do? (verse 6)

3. From 1 Chronicles 29:22-25, summarize what happened in Solomon's life.

4. First Chronicles then ends with the death of David. From David's final words recorded in 2 Samuel 23:3-4, describe what it is like for a nation to have a ruler who rules in righteousness.

5. Sometimes those in authority over us are righteous; sometimes they are not. Either way, what are we told to do in 1 Timothy 2:1-2, and why?

6. Personal: Although he fell into sin, David ruled over his people as a godly and righteous man. There are many who have a certain measure of authority over us, not just as the head of our government. Students have teachers, children have parents, employees have employers, etc. Make a list of those who are in some type of authority over you, and commit to pray for them.

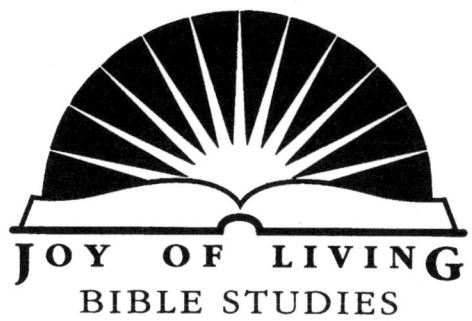
2 Samuel & 1 Chronicles — The King After God's Own Heart[1]

Since the books of 2 Samuel and 1 Chronicles cover the same period of time, even though from quite distinct viewpoints, and though they do not follow one another in the biblical order, they may be studied as one book. They both center upon the story of one man—David, the king "after [God's] own heart" (1 Samuel 13:14; Acts 13:22).

There are two ways that we may view David's life. First, he is a picture of the Lord Jesus Christ. David was not only a physical ancestor of Jesus, but like Jesus, David endured rejection and persecution. During his exile he gathered men around him who later, after he was king, became his commanders and generals. Thus David pictures Christ in His rejection—forsaken by the world, but gathering privately those who will be His commanders, generals, and captains when He comes to reign in power and glory over the earth.

Second, David is also a picture of each individual believer, and as we read about him, his triumphs and failures, these stories come alive and glow with truth for us. "These things...were written," Paul says, "as warnings for us" (1 Corinthians 10:11), that we might understand ourselves as we see events worked out in the lives of the characters in the Old Testament.

The story of David portrays what happens in a Christian's life as he follows God into the place of dominion. Every Christian is offered a kingdom, just as David was offered a kingdom. That kingdom is the believer's own life. There are enemies threatening it from the outside and from within, just as there were enemy nations outside the boundaries of Israel and enemy tribes living among the people within the land. The enemies from without picture for us the world and the direct attacks of the devil upon us. The enemies within represent those elements of the sinful nature that threaten to undermine the dominion that God intends us to have as we learn to reign in life by Jesus Christ. We do not call them Ammonites, Jebusites, etc., as they are called in the Old Testament; rather we call them jealousy, lust, bitterness, worry, etc. But they are the same enemies and proceed in the same ways.

David, was called "a man after [God's] own heart," but Saul, the first king of Israel, was a king "like all the other nations" (1 Samuel

8:20). As we saw in 1 Samuel, Saul represents the man of the sinful nature who tries in his own way to please God by good-intentioned, highly sincere, but basically disobedient efforts to be religious. For him everything falls apart. We learned from Saul that the Christian life is not to be a shabby imitation of the life of Jesus Christ. It must be the real thing, with Christ Himself living His life in us. As Saul was the picture of the sinful nature and its attempt to imitate reality, David is the picture of the believer in whom the Spirit of God dwells, who is open to the instruction of the Spirit, and who is led by the Spirit.

From Exile to the Throne (2 Samuel 1-5)

Second Samuel opens with a second account of the death of Saul. David learned of Saul's and Jonathan's death from a passing Amalekite, who boasted that he killed Saul, took his crown, and brought it to David. We can regard his tale as a fabrication, for it differs considerably from the account of the death of Saul in 1 Samuel. He probably found the dead body of the king and attempted to use it for his own advancement. David, however, honored Saul as the Lord's anointed, and gave the Amalekite the ultimate penalty.

David's first act after the death of Saul was to inquire of the Lord where he should establish his residence as king of Judah; God directed him to the city of Hebron. Here David was anointed as king by his own tribe of Judah. However, kingship over all 12 tribes was not to be easily gained, for Abner, the cousin of Saul and his leading general, took Ishbosheth, the 40-year-old son of Saul, and anointed him king over all Israel outside of Judah. This act precipitated warfare between David and the house of Saul, which broke out in immediate conflict between Abner and Joab, David's nephew and general over the fighting men of Judah. Both these men were strong and powerful leaders, and remained rivals throughout their careers.

The warfare between David and the house of Saul continued for seven years. Matters were brought to a crisis by a quarrel that broke out between Abner and King Ishbosheth. In anger Abner swore to transfer his loyalty to David and thus to carry out what he felt all along was God's purpose—to make David king over all Israel. But when Joab, David's general, learned that Abner, his hated rival, was about to become David's supporter, Joab killed Abner. King David denied all complicity with this murder, openly praised Abner to the people, and followed his bier to the grave. This greatly pleased the people, and David steadily won their respect, love and support for his kingship.

---

1. This is an overview. You can study this material in more detail in the Joy of Living study titled *2 Samuel*.

Two men of the tribe of Benjamin murdered Ishbosheth and brought his head to David, thinking to gain his approval, but he met them with the same treatment he had given the Amalekite who brought the news of Saul's death. Their immediate death at the hands of David's men demonstrated again David's unwillingness to make use of subterfuge and injustice to secure the ends appointed by God. Nevertheless, with the deaths of Abner and Ishbosheth, the warfare with the house of Saul was ended, and the way was now clear for David to be king over all of Israel. At no time did David take matters into his own hands. He was willing to wait for God's timing to fulfill His promises. Perhaps you are wondering when, or even if, God will fulfill His promises to you. Hebrews 10:35-36 says, "So do not throw away your confidence; it will be richly rewarded. You need to persevere so that when you have done the will of God, you will receive what he has promised."

The elders of all the tribes gathered at Hebron and there publicly acknowledged David as king over the entire land. His first act was to capture the city of Jerusalem, the home of the Jebusites (a Canaanite tribe), and make it his capital. Following this, he built a magnificent palace of cedar in Jerusalem. His growing power as king was immediately manifest in a double victory over the Philistine armies.

Worship and Victory (2 Samuel 6-10)

With the borders of the land secure, David felt the time had come to bring the ark back from its long resting place in Kiriath Jearim, also called Baalah of Judah. David built a new ox cart, set the ark in the middle of it, and started back to Jerusalem with the people singing and rejoicing. It was a time of enthusiastic, sincere, and complete devotion to God. But then a terrible thing happened: the oxen stumbled, and it looked as though the ark was about to fall off the cart. A man named Uzzah reached out his hand to steady it, and the moment his hand touched the ark, the wrath of God struck him dead.

Of course the rejoicing and merrymaking were abruptly stopped. David was so sick at heart that he turned the ox cart aside and put the Ark of God in the house of Obed-Edom. Then he returned to Jerusalem, bitter and resentful against the Lord for doing such a thing.

Although David was afraid of the Lord because of this event, the truth was that it was David's fault that Uzzah had died. In Exodus 25 and Numbers 4 there were very specific instructions on how the ark was to be moved. The priests were to cover it and the Levites were to carry it by its poles. No one was to touch it. It was David's fault that the Levites had not been asked to move the ark. David had to learn the lesson that sincerity in serving God is never enough. Things must be done God's way in accomplishing God's will.

Perhaps you have had some similar experience. You may have had some favorite project which you felt, in the earnestness of your heart, would be a wonderful thing to glorify God, and you set about it, determined to bring it to pass. But God failed to bless the project and the whole thing crumbled to pieces. The death of Uzzah stands as a constant testimony that it is not God's responsibility to carry out our program; it is rather our responsibility to be in such a relationship to Him that He may carry out His program through us.

After three months, during which the ark brought great blessing to the house of Obed-Edom, David had recovered to the point where he was ready to bring the ark into Jerusalem, borne properly upon the shoulders of the Levites. As he danced in joy before the ark he drew the contempt of his wife Michal, the daughter of Saul, who looked out at him from her window. But David was able to ignore her reproach, for he knew that what he had done was proper and right before God.

After David brought the ark back to Jerusalem, he was concerned that while he was dwelling in a beautiful palace of cedar, the ark rested in a lowly tent. It came into his heart to build a magnificent house for the Ark of God. When Nathan the prophet heard of this, he encouraged David to fulfill his desire. But God sent a message to Nathan saying that it was not His will for David to build Him a house, since he was a man of war and had shed so much blood on the earth; however, God would raise up one of David's sons, a man of peace, who could properly build the house of God. Though God had rejected his plan to build the house, David humbly accepted His will.

The rest of this section gives an account of David's consolidation of his kingdom, conquering many of Israel's enemies on every side. A beautiful interlude is recounted of David's search for any remaining sons of Jonathan. Upon finding one named Mephibosheth, who had been lamed by a fall on the terrible day when Saul and Jonathan fell in battle, David brought him to Jerusalem, set him at his own table, and treated him as his own son. Thus he remembered his covenant with Jonathan to show God's kindness to his descendants.

Failure and Forgiveness (2 Samuel 11-20)

The next part of the story of David tells of his tragic downfall and the entrance of sudden and terrible sin into his life. Walking on the roof of his palace (when he should have been with his army), David saw a beautiful woman taking a bath. He sent someone to find out about her, and then he sent for her and slept with her. In that sequence of events we see the process of temptation. All temptation begins, first, with a simple desire. The desire may be along any avenue, but whenever it appears, it must be properly dealt with. Either it is to be put away, or it is to be formed into a proper intent. David saw the woman, desired her, and then began to work out a way by which he could take her, even though he knew it was wrong. This was followed by an act of adultery, and David was thus involved in deep sin.

Instead of openly confessing and acknowledging the wrong and trying to make it right, David committed another sin to cover it up. This is often the process of sin. Commit one sin and you must commit another to cover that one up, and 10 more to cover up the second. So when David found out that Bathsheba was pregnant, he sent for her husband Uriah and tried to trick him into sleeping with his wife, to make it appear that the child she was carrying was Uriah's. But Uriah, in simple faithfulness to his duty and to God, confounded David's plan. The matter ended finally in the murder of Uriah at the hands of the Ammonites. Joab, David's ruthless general, became a conspirator with David in the plot, and Uriah was placed at the forefront of battle. Though he was killed by the Ammonites, it was really David who was the murderer. So, suddenly and appallingly, there breaks into David's life the double sin of adultery and murder.

Many have wondered how the man who is called "a man after [God's] own heart" could ever merit such a title after being guilty of such sins. But look at what happened when God sent Nathan the prophet to him. Nathan told the king a parable which caught him completely off guard, and when the king responded in righteous anger, Nathan charged him with having committed the sin he had just condemned. Immediately David acknowledged his sin; he no longer tried to justify it, but confessed his guilt. It was at this point that David wrote Psalm 51. Many have turned to this psalm in times of guilt and self-condemnation, and have found in David's experience the grace to handle their own sin properly before God, and to know also the washing away of stain and ugliness in the ever-flowing stream of God's mercy.

Although God forgave and removed David's sin, there were still consequences. Nathan told David, "This is what the LORD says: 'Out of your own household I am going to bring calamity upon you. Before your very eyes I will take your wives and give them to one who is close to you, and he will lie with your wives in broad daylight'" (2 Samuel 12:11). This was eventually fulfilled by Absalom, David's own son. Nathan further said to the king, "But because by doing this you have made the enemies of the LORD show utter contempt, the son born to you will die" (2 Samuel 12:14). So it proved to be. The baby born of this illegitimate union died, even though David pleaded with the Lord in a poignant passage which reflects the tearing of his heart by grief. In all of this David accepted God's judgment without complaint, and was grateful for His mercy.

Second Samuel 13 tells the dark story of Amnon, David's son, who raped his own sister, Tamar. This resulted in a black hatred born in Absalom, also David's son, against Amnon. In David's family, among his own sons, was spread a bitter spirit of rebellion and evil created by David's personal failure. The story of Amnon and his quarrel with Absalom, and finally the murder of Absalom at the hand of Joab, shows King David to be utterly helpless. He could not even rebuke his own son, for Amnon simply followed in David's footsteps.

We are told next of the uprising of Absalom. This handsome son of David fomented rebellion throughout the whole kingdom and secretly worked against his father in attempting to take the throne for himself. He was so successful that David, along with all his court, finally had to flee Jerusalem. Weeping, David left the city, barefoot and with his head covered as a symbol of his penitent heart. He acknowledged the fact that these evil circumstances were the result of his own folly.

Meanwhile, back at Jerusalem, David's friend Hushai had won the confidence of Absalom and was invited to act as one of his counselors. Ahithophel, formerly David's advisor, suggested to Absalom that he immediately pursue and kill his father. Hushai was able to turn Absalom from such counsel and advised him to wait until he could gather a large army from all of Israel and then go up against the king. In suggesting this, he was seeking to give David time to gather men.

Eventually the two forces met in the forest of Ephraim, and a mighty conflict ensued, resulting in the death of over 20,000 men.

When Absalom saw that his forces were defeated, he tried to escape on a mule through the forest. His head was caught in the thick branches of a large oak, and he was left hanging in midair. When Joab heard of this, he immediately went to the spot and, taking three javelins, thrust them into Absalom's heart, directly contravening the orders of David, who had commanded his men to spare Absalom's life.

When the news of Absalom's death was brought to David, he was crushed with sorrow. Joab ultimately reproved him for his mourning and warned him that he was in danger of losing the support of his men by apparently loving his rebel son above all his loyal supporters.

David returned in triumph to Jerusalem. Through much humiliation, shame, and bloodshed, he was restored to his position as king, and the affairs of the kingdom were once again set in order.

The Epilogue (2 Samuel 21-24)

This section gathers up, though not in chronological order, some of the events which David experienced through his 40-year reign. The first is the story of the Gibeonites whom Saul had attacked, contrary to the covenant which Joshua had made with them when he first conquered the land. The result of Saul's breach of faith was a continuing famine in that section of the country, which could not be ended until expiation was made by handing over to the Gibeonites seven of Saul's descendants. The lesson of this incident is that the past must be reckoned with. If there are things in our past which can still be corrected, we have a responsibility before God to set these things straight.

Second Samuel 22 records one of David's most beautiful psalms. It appears again as Psalm 18. In it is found David's recognition of the things that made for greatness in his kingdom. He acknowledged God as the source of all human strength and as the One who alone can bring deliverance. He stated that what a person is to God, God will also be to that person. If one is open and honest with God, He will also be open and honest in return. But if a person insists on being crooked and deceitful, God will cause the circumstances of that person's life to deceive him or her.

The final chapter gives the account of David's sin of numbering Israel. Many have wondered why God would view this as sin, since He Himself had commanded Moses to number the people, as recorded in the book of Numbers. But David's numbering was done from a quite different motive, as seen in the rebuke of Joab to the king. Apparently the king began to reckon on his military might and the numbers of the people rather than wholly on the grace and power of God. For his sin, David was given a choice of three possible punishments; wisely, he left the matter in the hands of the Lord. To indicate the seriousness of reliance on human strength, the angel of the Lord was sent among Israel for three days, and a plague took the lives of 70,000 men. The prophet Gad was sent to the king to tell him to erect an altar on the threshing floor of Araunah the Jebusite, where the plague had ended. This was later to be the site of the temple in Jerusalem. Thus 2 Samuel closes with the man after God's own heart turning from his sin to the worship of the living God.

First Chronicles

First Chronicles was written after the return of Israel from their 70 years of captivity in Babylon. It was probably written by Ezra the priest, who also wrote the book of Ezra. He returned with the captives to reestablish the temple and the worship of God in Jerusalem.

Although 1 Chronicles covers much of the same period as 2 Samuel, it does so with a particular emphasis on the worship of Israel. The first nine chapters are given over to a long list of genealogies. If we look at these names carefully and compare them with other accounts, we will see that God is selecting and rejecting, excluding and including, and working toward an ultimate goal.

The genealogy begins at the dawn of human history, listing the descendants of Adam. Among the sons of Adam were Cain, Abel and Seth, but here Cain and Abel are excluded and the focus is upon the descendants of Seth, for from him eventually came the family of Abraham and the Israelites (from whom the Savior, Jesus Christ would come). Then the line of Seth is traced down to Enoch and Noah. The three sons of Noah are listed as Shem, Ham and Japheth, but Ham and Japheth are dismissed with a brief word and attention is focused on the line of Shem. From Shem we trace on down to Abraham and his family. The constant narrowing process also excludes Ishmael, son of Abraham, and Esau, son of Isaac, and focuses on Jacob's 12 sons who became the fathers of the 12 tribes of Israel. The genealogy continues and selects the tribes of Judah and Levi—the kingly and the priestly lines. It traces the tribe of Judah down to David, to Solomon, and then through the kings of the house of David to the Babylonian captivity. The tribe of Levi is traced down to Aaron, the first of the priests, and then to the priests at the time of David. Wherever God can find an obedient heart, that individual is included in the account. When God excludes a name, or turns from a line or family, it is always on the basis of repeated disobedience.

First Chronicles 10 gives a brief account of the death of Saul, and verses 13-14 tell why his kingship ended: "Saul died because he was unfaithful to the Lᴏʀᴅ; he did not keep the word of the Lᴏʀᴅ, and even consulted a medium for guidance, and did not inquire of the Lᴏʀᴅ."

God's King

The rest of 1 Chronicles is about David, emphasizing that from the moment he was anointed king, he was God's king. His first act after becoming king in Israel was to take over the pagan stronghold of the Jebusites, the city of Jerusalem—God's city. This was the place where God had chosen to put His name among the tribes of Israel.

Beginning with 1 Chronicles 11:10, the account names those who were loyal to David during his exile, and the things they did that made them mighty. These men eventually became leaders in his kingdom. It is a beautiful picture of the glory we will share with the Lord Jesus when He establishes His kingdom of righteousness over all the earth.

A second emphasis of the book is on the Ark of God. In 1 Chronicles 13-15 we find a retelling of David's bringing the ark to Jerusalem.

The restoration of the ark to the center of Israel's life was an occasion of great rejoicing, and we find in chapter 16 the great psalm sung on this momentous occasion. It is a great declaration of the government of God, of the majesty of God which draws forth the worship of His people, and of gratitude to God for what He is in Himself.

David's sin in numbering Israel is recounted as a departure from the principle of dependence upon the strength and glory of God. David desired to see the number of people that were available to him, and thus to glory in the physical strength of his realm. One of the great principles which runs through the Bible is that God never wins His battles by a majority. When we begin to think that the cause of Christ is losing out because the number of Christians is decreasing in proportion to the population of the world, we have succumbed to the false philosophy that God wins His battles by numbers.

Authority of the Temple

First Chronicles 22-29 tells of David's passion for the building of the temple. David longed to see the temple built. Though David knew that Solomon, his son, had been appointed by God to be the actual builder, yet in grace God allowed David to do everything for the temple except to actually build it. It was David who drew the plans, designed the furniture, collected the materials, and made all the arrangements for ritual and ceremony. When it was all ready, David commanded the leaders of Israel to help Solomon in his task when the time came.

Careful detail is given as to the work of the Levites in carrying out the work in the temple, and special attention is paid to the ministry of music for the services within the temple. David's musical skill had played a great part in his life, and his interest in these musical arrangements was most natural and delightful. David's concern for every detail of the building of the temple is evident in his care for the workers who labored in its building, and for the cultivation of crops and the raising of cattle and all that pertained to the welfare of his people in carrying out their central activity—the worship of the living God.

First Chronicles 28-29 recounts the final charge of David to his son Solomon. Then, David blessed the Lord in the presence of all the people, recognizing God's gracious gifts to them and the privilege of giving back to Him the very best that men could give. He concluded with a great prayer for Solomon, that God would preserve him in safety and grant him a perfect heart to fulfill the great work.

What is the ultimate message of 1 Chronicles? It is the supreme authority of the Lord in our individual life. Central to all of life is the worship of the heart. Over the three great doors of the cathedral in Milan, Italy, are three inscriptions. Over the right hand door is carved, "All that pleases is but for a moment." On the left hand door is, "All that troubles is but for a moment." Over the main entrance are the words, "Nothing is important save that which is eternal." This is the lesson of Chronicles, as it is the lesson of the whole Bible. "And whatever you do, whether in word or deed, do it all in the name of the Lord Jesus, giving thanks to God the Father through him" (Colossians 3:17).

Study Questions

Before you begin your study this week:
- ➢ Pray and ask God to speak to you through His Holy Spirit.
- ➢ Use only the Bible for your answers.
- ➢ Write down your answers and the verses you used.
- ➢ Answer the "Challenge" questions if you have the time and want to do them.
- ➢ Share your answers to the "Personal" questions with the class only if you want to share them.

First Day: Read the Commentary on 2 Samuel and 1 Chronicles.

1. What meaningful or new thought did you find in the Commentary on 2 Samuel and 1 Chronicles, or from your teacher's lecture? What personal application did you choose to apply to your life?

2. Look for a verse in the lesson to memorize this week. Write it down, carry it with you, tack it to your bulletin board, on the dashboard of your car, etc. Make a real effort to learn the verse and its "address" (reference of where it is found in the Bible).

3. This week's questions focus on 1 Kings and 2 Chronicles 1-20. If you have time, you may want to read through both this week. As you answer the questions, you will be looking up passages of Scripture from various places in the Bible. This will help you discover that God's Word is a "whole," and that His message to us is the same from Genesis to Revelation.

Since 1 Kings and 2 Chronicles 1-20 cover the same period of time, we will study them together. The writers of these books not only wrote books of history, but also chose significant events that would help readers understand the internal meaning of the outward events, especially as measured against the covenants which God made with Israel centuries before at Mount Sinai.

Second Day:

1. a. As the book of 1 Kings opens, mighty King David is now a feeble old man. Read 1 Kings 1:5. Who attempted to take David's throne?

   b. Who did David plan to be king after him? (1 Kings 1:28-30)

2. a. Read 1 Kings 2:1-4. What charge did David give to Solomon? (verses 1-3a)

   b. What would be the result of Solomon's obedience? (verses 3b-4)

3. a. Read 1 Kings 3:5-14. What did God offer Solomon? (verse 5)

   b. What did Solomon ask for? (verses 7-9)

   c. What did God give him? (verses 11-14)

4. a. God is able to give us all and more than we can imagine. You may think, "I wish God would offer me what He offered Solomon!" Summarize what Luke 12:15 and 1 Timothy 6:9-10 say about money and material goods.

b. Instead of pursuing wealth, what should the person of God pursue? Read 1 Timothy 6:11.

5. Personal: Take a few moments and search your own heart. What are you pursuing? How do you feel about money?

Third Day:

1. a. Solomon was a magnificent king! Read 1 Kings 4:20-28, and briefly describe Solomon's reign.

    b. From 1 Kings 4:29-34, briefly describe Solomon's wisdom.

2. a. From 1 Kings 5:5, what did Solomon intend to do?

    b. From 1 Kings 6:37-38, did he accomplish what he intended to do?

3. Despite God's gifts to Solomon and the magnificence of his reign, Solomon was still only a human being. His human weakness is noted for the first time in his alliance with the king of Egypt through his marriage to Pharaoh's daughter. When Solomon brought Pharaoh's daughter into his court, the door was opened for marriage alliances with other peoples. Soon he had 1,000 wives, and along with them came their idols. Read Exodus 34:15-16 and Deuteronomy 17:16-17, and compare what God said to what Solomon did.

4. a. Read 1 Kings 11:4-8. Solomon disobeyed God by marrying many foreign women. What did that disobedience lead him to do?

    b. How did God respond to Solomon's actions? (1 Kings 11:9-13, summarize briefly)

5. Personal: Solomon began well. He had every blessing and opportunity, but he compromised in one area, and that led to his downfall. Read 1 Corinthians 10:12-13, Ephesians 4:27, and 1 Peter 5:8, and write down the warning in each. How will you apply them to your life?

Fourth Day:

The Lord raised up several adversaries against Solomon, including Jeroboam son of Nebat, an Ephraimite who rebelled against the king. God sent the prophet Ahijah to meet Jeroboam.

1. a. From 1 Kings 11:29-36, summarize what the Lord said to Jeroboam through Ahijah the prophet.

   b. What conditional promise did God give to Jeroboam, and what was the condition? (1 Kings 11:37-39)

2. a. After forty years of unprecedented magnificence, Solomon died and was buried in the City of David, a tragic close to a life which had begun with great promise. Because Solomon's son Rehoboam, in his pride, told the people that their burdens would be increased under his reign, the ten northern tribes revolted and chose Jeroboam to be their king, fulfilling the decree God had made to Solomon. Read 1 Kings 12:25-33. What great sin did Jeroboam introduce into the northern kingdom of Israel?[1]

   b. From 1 Kings 14:7-11, what did God have to say about Jeroboam, and what judgment did God pronounce on him?

3. From 1 Kings 14:21-30, describe briefly what transpired in Judah under Rehoboam's reign.

4. a. David and Jeroboam became the standards of measurement for the kings that followed. From 1 Kings 15:9-11 and 2 Chronicles 29:1-2, how was a good king in the southern kingdom of Judah described?

   b. How was an evil king in the northern kingdom of Israel described om 1 Kings 15:33-34; 16:1-2; and 16:18-19?

5. Personal: Take stock of your own life. Do you do what is "right in the eyes of the Lord," or does your life reflect Jeroboam's—sinning and causing others to fall into sin?

Fifth Day:

The kingdom of God's people remained divided. In the southern kingdom, Judah, there were a few godly kings among many who were evil. In the northern kingdom, Israel, there was never a godly king, just a continual succession of kings who walked in idolatrous ways. Despite this, God, in grace, often intervened by sending prophets to arrest the decay and fall of the northern kingdom.

1. From 1 Kings 16:29-33, briefly describe who Ahab was, what he was like, and what he did.

2. a. In 1 Kings 17:1 we are introduced to the great and mighty prophet, Elijah the Tishbite, who was used by God to repeatedly confront Ahab and the people of Israel with their wickedness and their need to repent or face God's judgment. Read 1 Kings 18:18-39, which tells of one confrontation. Who was to meet on Mount Carmel? (verses 18-20)

   b. From verses 21-25, summarize Elijah's challenge.

   c. From verses 26-38, summarize what took place.

   d. From verse 39, how did the people respond?

---

1. The northern kingdom of 10 tribes, under Jeroboam, was known as Israel. The southern kingdom of 2 tribes, under Rehoboam, was known as Judah. See chart on page 8 for a list of the subsequent rulers of Israel and of Judah.

3. a. God did amazing miracles through Elijah, but the prophet was still a human being. Read 1 Kings 19:9-10. What were Elijah's concerns?

   b. How did God encourage Elijah? (1 Kings 19:11-12, 15-18, summarize briefly)

4. Personal: God didn't remove Elijah's difficulties; in fact, He gave him a new assignment, including training his eventual replacement. God did meet with and speak to Elijah. Are you facing difficult circumstances? Take time out to be alone with God. He may or may not change your circumstances, but He will change you and strengthen you to face whatever comes your way.

Sixth Day:

Second Chronicles focuses on the spiritual deeds and misdeeds of the kings. There were many ungodly kings of Judah; however, the few good ones shone as lights in the darkness.

1. Read 2 Chronicles 15:1-7. Summarize the message God sent to king Asa of Judah through Azariah.

2. a. From 2 Chronicles 15:8-18, list Asa's actions that show he believed God.

   b. From 2 Chronicles 15:15a, how did the people respond to Asa's reforms?

   c. From 2 Chronicles 15:15b, what did God do for the people?

3. a. What problem arose for Jehoshaphat king of Judah, and what did he and the people of Judah do? (2 Chronicles 20:1-13, summarize)

   b. Challenge: What did Solomon pray in 2 Chronicles 6:28-31, and what did God promise in 2 Chronicles 7:14? How do these principles relate to the action of Jehoshaphat and the people of Judah?

4. What encouragement did the Lord give to them? (2 Chronicles 20:14-15)

5. a. Read 2 Chronicles 20:16-27. What action were the people to take? (verses 16-17)

   b. What did God do as the people sang and praised? (verses 20-24, summarize briefly)

   c. How did the people respond? (verses 26-27)

6. Personal: What battle are you facing in life? What have you learned today that will help you deal with it?

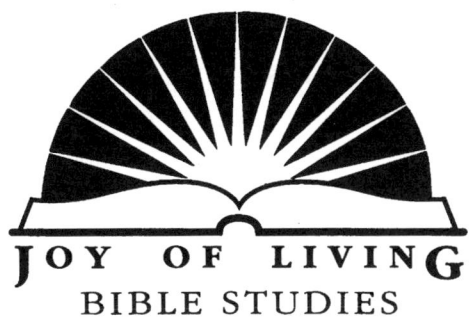

JOY OF LIVING
BIBLE STUDIES

1st Kings & 2nd Chronicles 1-20 — The Way to Lose a Kingdom

In the Hebrew Bible, our books of 1 and 2 Kings are combined into one book simply called Kings. The division was made in the first century before Christ by the translators of the Greek version of the Old Testament. Since 1 Kings and 2 Chronicles 1-20 cover the same period of time, we will study them together. The unknown writers of these books not only wrote a book of history, but also selectively chose significant events that would help readers understand the internal meaning of the outward events, especially as measured against the covenants which God made with Israel centuries before at Mount Sinai.

First Kings begins with the reign of Solomon and the tragic division of the kingdom under his son Rehoboam. Then we are given summaries of the various dynasties within the northern kingdom of Israel, and the lives of the kings of the single dynasty of the house of David in the southern kingdom of Judah.[1] In each case, the spotlight is always on the king, for it was what the king did in relationship to God that determined how the nation went. When the king walked with God in obedience and humility, God's blessing rested upon the kingdom. But when the king disobeyed and allowed the people to worship other gods, famines, plagues, and invasions occurred.

The kingdom of Israel pictures our own lives. God chose Israel to be a nation and gave it its unique laws and its unique government in order to provide an example to all the world of what the living God is willing to be in any individual's life. As we read these books, we find ourselves also in the midst of the problems, the blessings, and the possibilities that are reflected in these books of the kings.

The Reign of Solomon (1 Kings 1-11)

First Kings opens with the last days of David. He appears here as a very old and feeble man, unable to discharge properly the duties of his high office. This feebleness created the opportunity for one of his sons, Adonijah, to foment a rebellion which would make him the successor to his father. Though Adonijah obtained the support of Joab and Abiathar the priest, his plans were thwarted by the intervention of Nathan the prophet who, through Bathsheba, David's wife and Solomon's mother, informed King David of the plot. Immediately David arranged for the public anointing of Solomon as king.

Adonijah, fearing Solomon, took shelter at the altar in the court of the tabernacle and was spared for a season. After David's death, Adonijah presumed to threaten the throne by seeking marriage with the girl who had been David's caregiver during the closing days of his life, and for this he was executed at Solomon's command.

Before David died, he solemnly charged Solomon to walk in the ways of the Lord and to teach his children, that the kingdom might endure in safety and prosperity forever. The reign of Solomon appeared to hold much promise, for he loved the Lord and walked according to the statutes of his father David. Soon after Solomon ascended the throne, the Lord appeared to him in a dream and offered him his choice of gifts. The young king asked for a discerning heart in order to govern God's people—he wanted the ability to distinguish between good and evil, right and wrong. God not only gave Solomon what he asked, but added also the riches and honor he might have chosen but wisely had passed by. It is evident from this that wealth and fame are proper honors when God bestows them, but if sought for selfish purposes, they frequently prove to be curses rather than blessings.

Solomon's gift of wisdom was manifested in the famous story of his choice between two mothers who each claimed a certain baby as her own. When Solomon ordered the child divided by a sword and half given to each, the real mother quickly gave up her right in order that the child might live, though the other woman would possess it. Solomon promptly awarded the child to the first and true mother. With this incident his fame spread throughout the kingdom and far beyond.

Despite God's gifts to Solomon and the magnificence of his reign, a note of weakness is first noted in his alliance with the king of Egypt through his marriage to Pharaoh's daughter. Egypt in the Scripture is always a picture of the world's allurement. When Solomon brought Pharaoh's daughter into his court, the door was opened for marriage alliances with other peoples. Soon he had 1,000 wives, and along with them came their idols. Thus, despite outward prosperity and glory, the kingdom began to deteriorate under Solomon because he allowed the world to entice him and draw him away from the Lord.

By the fourth year of his reign, Solomon was ready to begin building the temple. The stones for the temple were finished within the quarry so that "no hammer, chisel or any other iron tool was heard at the temple site while it was being built" (1 Kings 6:7). This process finds its parallel in Paul's statement in Ephesians 2:20-22 concerning the building of the church. It is "built on the foundation of the apostles and prophets, with Christ Jesus himself as the chief cornerstone. In

1. See chart on page 8 for a list of the rulers of Israel and of Judah.

him the whole building is joined together and rises to become a holy temple in the Lord. And in him you too are being built together to become a dwelling in which God lives by his Spirit." Without noise or fanfare the Spirit of God is constructing a glorious temple, from living materials, to be a habitation of God.

Solomon built the temple along the same pattern as the tabernacle, though it was double the size and was both more magnificent and more durable. Like the tabernacle, the temple was most beautiful within, for almost everything was covered with pure gold.

In the midst of the account of the building of the temple, which took seven years, the writer interjects a brief account of the building of Solomon's palace, and adds: "It took Solomon thirteen years, however, to complete the construction of his palace" (1 Kings 7:1). The significance of this is seen in the insightful comment of Dr. G. Campbell Morgan, "If the time and possessions devoted to our own comfort be greater than those devoted to the service of God, it is sure proof that the master passion is self-centered rather than God-centered."

At the dedication of the temple, the sacred furnishings were installed within the temple. After the priests placed the ark in the Most Holy Place, a cloud of glory from the Lord filled the temple. Solomon, standing before the altar of burnt offering and raising his hands toward heaven, gave a prayer of dedication, recognizing the faithfulness of God and the peril of departing from His ways. Solomon's understanding of God's transcendent majesty was manifest in his words, "But will God really dwell on earth? The heavens, even the highest heaven, cannot contain you. How much less this temple I have built!" (1 Kings 8:27). Following this, thousands of sacrifices were offered. At the close, the joyful people returned to their homes, having participated in the greatest moment of glory the nation was to know, from the days of Moses until the time of the Messiah.

God appeared again to Solomon in a dream. He told Solomon that His promises to David his father were renewed, upon the condition that Solomon and his descendants would walk faithfully before the Lord. If they failed to do this, the temple would be torn down, and the people would be driven from the land and become an object of ridicule. As we read the account, we know the terrible fulfillment of this in history, for the conditions were not kept either by the king or the people, so that the penalty was fulfilled in precise detail.

At the apex of Solomon's prosperity the famous visit of the queen of Sheba[1] occurred. Sheba is believed to have been located in what is now Yemen. Even at that distance its queen had heard of Solomon, especially of his wisdom and blessing from the Most High God. She came to Jerusalem to see for herself whether what she had heard was true. When Solomon showed her the magnificence of his palace and of his kingdom, she reported that even the half had not been told her, but in words of great insight she said that his greatness was because of God, "Praise be to the LORD your God, who has delighted in you and placed you on the throne of Israel. Because of the LORD's eternal love for Israel, he has made you king, to maintain justice and righteousness" (1 Kings 10:9).

In 1 Kings 11 the writer unveils the degeneration within Solomon's heart which was soon to result in the division of his kingdom. The point where evil first took hold was in Solomon's love for women. He let his heart go after women from nations with which the Lord had forbidden the Israelites to enter into marriage. Soon he built temples for these women to practice idolatry, and eventually he joined them there, actually bowing down himself to the abominable idols of his pagan wives. For this, "The LORD became angry with Solomon because his heart had turned away from the LORD, the God of Israel, who had appeared to him twice" (1 Kings 11:9). For the third time God appeared to Solomon, this time to announce to him that the kingdom would be torn from him and given to another; yet for David's sake it would occur after Solomon died, during the lifetime of Solomon's son.

Several adversaries rose up against Solomon, including Jeroboam son of Nebat, an Ephraimite who rebelled against the king. God sent the prophet Ahijah to meet Jeroboam. Ahijah tore his new cloak into twelve pieces, and handed Jeroboam ten, symbolizing that Jeroboam would be given ten of the twelve tribes, while only two—Judah and Benjamin—would remain with the house of David. The promise of God's blessing given to David was extended to Jeroboam if he, too, would walk in the ways of God and keep His commands. When Solomon heard of this he tried to kill Jeroboam, who fled into Egypt and remained there until Solomon died. After forty years of unprecedented magnificence, Solomon died and was buried in the City of David, a tragic close to a life which had begun with great promise.

The life of Solomon indicates the importance of the human will. In the kingdom of your life your will is king, and nothing can take place in that kingdom except as it is allowed by the choice of your will. If you yield yourself obediently to the influence of the Holy Spirit dwelling in you, you are like the kingdom when David walked with God and the land flourished. But if, like Solomon, you begin to walk in disobedience, then evil invasions will begin in your life. You will no longer have strength to repel inward corruptions that take their toll upon you; thus the kingdom of your life will fall into ruin as well.

The Division of the Kingdom (1 Kings 12-16)

When Solomon's son Rehoboam came to Shechem to be anointed king, the people, led by Jeroboam (who had returned from Egypt), asked that he would grant them relief from many of the burdens which Solomon had placed upon them, including forced labor and heavy taxation. Rehoboam, in his pride, told the people that their burdens would be increased. The ten tribes revolted and chose Jeroboam to be their king, fulfilling the decree God had made to Solomon.

Jeroboam set up his capital at Shechem and, fearing that if the people continued to worship at Jerusalem they would eventually return to the authority of Rehoboam, he introduced the great sin for which the northern kingdom was ever after to be noted. Making two golden calves, he set one up in Dan and another in Bethel, saying, "Here are your gods, O Israel" (1 Kings 12:28).

From this moment on in Israel's history, David and Jeroboam became representative of two spiritual principles that are traced through-

---

1. Although some have said there was a sexual relationship between the Queen of Sheba and Solomon, there is no biblical reference to this.

out the kingdoms. They became the standards of measurement for the kings that followed. In Judah it was said of a good king that he "did what was right in the eyes of the Lord, as his father David had done" (1 Kings 15:11); but in the northern kingdom, it was said of an evil king that he "did evil in the eyes of the Lord, walking in the ways of Jeroboam" (1 Kings 15:34). It is significant that in Israel, the northern kingdom, there were no godly kings at all, but a continual succession of kings who walked in idolatrous ways and who frequently gained the throne by murdering their predecessors. Despite this, God in grace often intervened by sending prophets to arrest the decay and fall of the northern kingdom. In Judah, the southern kingdom, there were a few godly kings among many who were evil, but these stood out like lights in the darkness—Asa, Jehoshaphat, Joash, Hezekiah and Josiah.

In an attempt to give Jeroboam opportunity for repentance, God sent a prophet to him, warning him of his evil by predicting the immediate destruction of the altar at Bethel. When Jeroboam stretched out his hand to order the prophet's arrest, his hand shriveled up, and he could not pull it back. When he begged the prophet for healing, his hand was restored, but there was no real repentance on Jeroboam's part. Further judgment fell upon Jeroboam. The prophet Ahijah sent word to him that the same God who had exalted him to power and made him king over Israel would now, because of his sin, remove him from the throne. The sign of it would be that his son Abijah would die, and the sign was fulfilled. Nothing further is told us concerning the 22 years of the reign of Jeroboam except the record of his death and the fact that his son Nadab reigned in his stead.

Meanwhile, things were going no better in the southern kingdom under Rehoboam, whose 17-year reign also was characterized by idolatry. The result was an invasion by the king of Egypt, who carried away the treasures of gold from the temple and the king's palace. The substitution of bronze shields and vessels for the golden ones was God's reminder to the king of the deterioration of the worship in the land. Rehoboam, too, rested with his fathers and was buried in the City of David, and Abijah, his son, succeeded him as king.

Abijah lasted three years as king of Judah before he died, and one of the good kings, Asa, began a 41-year reign. Asa's reforms included the removal of idols, even the Asherah pole belonging to his grandmother, whom he removed from her office because of her idolatry. This partial reform under Asa undoubtedly preserved Judah, for a time, from the corruption which was evident in the northern kingdom.

Elijah: The Prophet of Fire (1 Kings 17-22)

The northern kingdom suffered under the rule of a series of evil kings. All this time, God tried to reach His people in Israel. When the most evil of all the kings of the northern kingdom ascended the throne, we meet a prophet whose name rings through history.

King Ahab of Israel not only adopted the idolatry of Jeroboam but also married Jezebel, the daughter of the king of Sidon, and thus introduced the worship of Baal into Israel. He "did more to provoke the Lord, the God of Israel, to anger than did all the kings of Israel before him" (1 Kings 16:33). It was during the reign of this evil pair that the prophet Elijah appeared, bringing to mind the declaration of Romans 5:20, "Where sin increased, grace increased all the more."

Elijah came from Gilead, east of the Jordan, but not much more is known of his background. He suddenly confronted Ahab with the announcement that God was about to bring a severe drought upon the land, which would not be relieved until Elijah gave the word. To protect Elijah from the wrath of Ahab, God sent him first to the Kerith Ravine, east of the Jordan, where he was fed by ravens, and then to the land of Sidon on the coast, where he lived with a widow and her son.

After three years Elijah was sent back to Ahab, who greeted him with the words, "Is that you, you troubler of Israel?" (1 Kings 18:17). Elijah responded that it was the king who, through his idolatry, had troubled the land. Elijah then challenged Ahab to a contest to be held on Mount Carmel. As the contest began all the people of Israel, including 450 prophets of Baal and 400 prophets of Asherah, gathered. Elijah cried out to the people, "If the Lord is God, follow him; but if Baal is God, follow him" (1 Kings 18:21). The people said nothing, so Elijah laid out the rules of the contest: "Get two bulls for us. Let [the prophets of Baal] choose one for themselves, and let them cut it into pieces and put it on the wood but not set fire to it. I will prepare the other bull and put it on the wood but not set fire to it. Then you call on the name of your god, and I will call on the name of the Lord. The god who answers by fire—he is God" (1 Kings 18:23-24).

The prophets of Baal called out in vain for Baal to burn up the sacrifice that waited on the altar. Elijah mocked them by suggesting that perhaps the god was asleep, deep in thought, busy, or traveling. Finally it was Elijah's turn, and after drenching his sacrifice with water, he prayed. God answered by sending fire from heaven to burn up not only the sacrifice, but also the wood, the stones and the soil of the altar, and the water in the trench. The people responded by falling on their faces, crying out, "The Lord—He is God! The Lord—He is God!" (1 Kings 18:39). The prophets of Baal were put to death at Elijah's command, and soon after the rain came in great torrents in answer to Elijah's prayer (see James 5:17-18).

The furious Jezebel sent a message to Elijah threatening him with immediate death. Surprisingly, the prophet who stood with great courage against 850 adversaries on Mount Carmel now fled for his life from a single woman. But God, with patience and tender care, first met Elijah's physical need and then sent him to Mount Horeb, where He revealed Himself to Elijah in "a gentle whisper" (1 Kings 19:12). That quiet voice then rebuked him for his lack of faith and revealed to him that there were yet 7,000 within the nation of Israel who had not bowed the knee to Baal. Elijah was sent back to anoint Hazael to be king of Aram, Jehu to be king of Israel, and Elisha to succeed him as prophet. The obedient prophet returned and, finding Elisha plowing, threw his cloak around him. After offering a sacrifice, Elisha took up his new role as servant to the old prophet.

Despite Ahab's wickedness, God's mercy was extended to him when Ben-Hadaad, king of Aram, attacked. Ben-Hadad demanded the surrender of the city of Samaria but, through an unnamed prophet, God announced the defeat of the Arameans by Israel. The Arameans again attacked the following spring. Once again Israel won by the mercy and grace of God. But in the moment of his triumph, Ahab made a covenant with Ben-Hadad, whom God had clearly determined should die. For this, God sent a prophet again to Ahab to announce his doom.

The terrible struggle between good and evil in the heart of King Ahab seemed to reach its crisis in the account of his selfish longing to possess the vineyard of his neighbor, Naboth, who refused to sell it. Falsely charging Naboth with having cursed God and the king, Jezebel obtained his death by stoning at the hands of the citizens of the city. But when Ahab went to the vineyard to take possession, he was confronted by Elijah, who told him that his dynasty would end. Ahab tore his clothes and, with fasting and sackcloth, expressed his repentance. It was enough to obtain a temporary reprieve. God said, "I will bring [this disaster] on his house in the days of his son" (1 Kings 21:29).

The final chapter in the book of 1 Kings details the visit of Jehoshaphat of Judah in order to establish an alliance with Ahab of Israel. Planning war against Aram, Ahab invited Jehoshaphat to accompany him. The two kings sought the counsel of God as to the outcome of the battle. Four hundred false prophets attached to Ahab's court promised success, but Jehoshaphat insisted on consulting Micaiah, a true prophet of God in Israel. At first Micaiah gave an ironic confirmation of the prediction of victory, but when pressed he gave the true word of the Lord, predicting the death of Ahab during the battle.

Ahab disguised himself and placed Jehoshaphat in a conspicuous place during the battle, hoping that Jehoshaphat would be mistaken for Ahab himself and be killed. But an arrow shot at random by a warrior on the opposite side found its way through Ahab's armor. God is the God of circumstances, and even of "accidents"! Ahab's body was brought to the capital where his bloodstained chariot was washed, and the dogs licked up his blood according to Elijah's prophecy.

The stories in 1 Kings picture for us the truth in Proverbs 4:23, "Above all else, guard your heart, for it is the wellspring of life." Those who allow any place, thing, or person to take the place in their heart that belongs only to God, have begun to alienate themselves from the life of God and all His blessings.

Second Chronicles 1-20

Chronicles gives us more detail of the worship of Israel and Judah and their kings than it does of historical matters. The transfer of worship from the tabernacle to the temple symbolizes the spiritual growth of a Christian. From our early up and down experiences, like Israel in the desert, we grow to a more settled condition where we recognize the Lord Jesus as King and walk more consistently in Him.

In building the temple, Solomon pictured Christ as the Prince of Peace, who has the honor of building the true temple of the Holy Spirit, the human body. In Hebrews 3:5-6 we are told, "Moses was faithful as a servant in all God's house...But Christ is faithful as a son over God's house. And we are his house." Christ is the One who has made the temple of our body, which contains the sanctuary of the Spirit.

The furniture of the temple, except for the Ark of the Covenant, was rebuilt completely. The ark, which symbolized the initial meeting

place of God and humanity, needed no duplication, for the new birth can never be repeated. But in other ways, the temple represented a new beginning. This parallels the experience of many Christians who, often after years of a vacillating experience, come to a place where they yield themselves anew to the Lordship of Christ.

The response of God to Solomon's dedication of the temple is given in somewhat fuller detail than the account in 1 Kings. Here the well-known promise is found in 2 Chronicles 7:14, "If my people, who are called by my name, will humble themselves and pray and seek my face and turn from their wicked ways, then will I hear from heaven and will forgive their sin and will heal their land."

The visit from the queen of Sheba to Solomon pictures the means by which God intended the whole earth to know the story of His grace. In the Old Testament, God's grace was displayed by the building of a people so blessed of God and so different from other nations, that word of it would spread. People would come to Jerusalem from all over to learn the secret of God's blessing. In the New Testament, every believer is to walk in obedience to the Spirit of God, who inhabits the temple of our human spirit. Our lives are to so manifest the victory, the rejoicing, the blessing, the prosperity, and the joy of the Lord, that people around will ask, "What is your secret?" As 1 Peter 3:15 puts it, "Always be prepared to give an answer to everyone who asks you to give the reason for the hope that you have."

During the reign of Solomon's son Rehoboam, despite his personal weakness, there was considerable spiritual vitality within Judah: "Those from every tribe of Israel who set their hearts on seeking the Lord, the God of Israel, followed the Levites to Jerusalem to offer sacrifices to the Lord, the God of their fathers. They strengthened the kingdom of Judah and supported Rehoboam son of Solomon for three years, walking in the ways of David and Solomon during this time" (2 Chronicles 11:16-17). Rehoboam misunderstood the secret of his strength and, it is later recorded: "He and all Israel with him abandoned the law of the Lord" (2 Chronicles 12:1). In judgment, Shishak king of Egypt came and carried off the treasures of the temple.

Further detail is also given regarding the reign of Jehoshaphat. Upon returning from the battle of Ramoth Gilead, where Ahab was killed, Jehoshaphat was rebuked by the prophet Jehu for having made an alliance with Ahab. Jehoshaphat responded by turning back to God. Soon after, Judah was threatened by an invasion. Jehoshaphat led the nation in prayer before the temple, confessing their powerlessness and their ignorance of what to do, and pleading with God for His intervention. God sent such confusion and terror among the enemy that they turned upon each other and their vast army was completely destroyed. Jehoshaphat reigned for 25 years, during which he had, for the most part, walked in godly ways.

Throughout these books we see that those who served the Lord encouraged those under their authority to also serve Him. Those kings who walked in unrighteousness and worshipped other gods paved the way for their entire nation to follow in their ungodly ways. Think of those in the sphere of your influence. Are you, by example, encouraging them to know, love, and serve the Lord, or are you paving the way for them to walk in unrighteousness?

Study Questions

Before you begin your study this week:
- ☙ Pray and ask God to speak to you through His Holy Spirit.
- ☙ Use only the Bible for your answers.
- ☙ Write down your answers and the verses you used.
- ☙ Answer the "Challenge" questions if you have the time and want to do them.
- ☙ Share your answers to the "Personal" questions with the class only if you want to share them.

First Day: Read the Commentary on 1 Kings and 2 Chronicles 1-20.

1. What meaningful or new thought did you find in the Commentary on 1 Kings and 2 Chronicles 1-20, or from your teacher's lecture? What personal application did you choose to apply to your life?

2. Look for a verse in the lesson to memorize this week. Write it down, carry it with you, tack it to your bulletin board, on the dashboard of your car, etc. Make a real effort to learn the verse and its "address" (reference of where it is found in the Bible).

3. This week's questions focus on 2 Kings and 2 Chronicles 21-36. If you have time, you may want to read through both this week. As you answer the questions, you will be looking up passages of Scripture from various places in the Bible. This will help you discover that God's Word is a "whole," and that His message to us is the same from Genesis to Revelation.

Second Kings continues the record of the kings of Judah and Israel[1] and of the continual downward spiral of both these kingdoms. In the opening chapter, at God's direction, the prophet Elijah rebuked Ahaziah, the evil king of Israel, and Ahaziah died according to God's word. His younger brother Joram, who was also evil, succeeded him.

Second Day:

At God's direction, Elisha had become Elijah's understudy and would eventually be his successor.

1. Read 2 Kings 2:1-5. What was about to happen? (verses 1, 3, 5)

2. a. Read 2 Kings 2:8-14. What did Elisha want Elijah to do for him? (verse 9)

   b. What happened to Elijah? (verse 11)

   c. How did Elisha know that his request had been granted? (verses 10, 12a, 14)

3. The series of incidents from the ministry of Elisha listed in 2 Kings indicates the grace and mercy extended to individuals even while the judgments of God brought about the ultimate overthrow and exile of the nation of Israel. Read 2 Kings 2:19-22. Summarize who had the problem, what the problem was, and how it was resolved.

---

1. See chart on page 8 for a list of the rulers of Israel and of Judah.

4. a. Moab rebelled against Israel's control, and King Joram of Israel was joined by King Jehoshaphat of Judah and by the king of Edom to suppress the rebellion. The allied kings found themselves in the desert with no water. They sought the counsel of Elisha. Read 2 Kings 3:14-25. What was the only reason Elisha was willing to help them? (verse 14)

    b. What instructions were they given? (verses 15-19, summarize briefly)

    c. What was the result of their obedience? (verses 20-25, summarize briefly)

5. Personal: If you would like to, share with the class a time when you were obedient to God's direction and what the result was.

Third Day:

We will continue to see God's mercy and grace shown to individuals.

1. a. Read 2 Kings 4:1-7. What was the problem? (verse 1)

    b. How it was resolved? (verses 2-7, summarize briefly)

2. a. Read 2 Kings 4:18-37. What was the problem? (verses 18-20)

    b. How was it was resolved? (verses 21-37, summarize briefly)

3. a. Read 2 Kings 4:38-41. Who had the problem, and what was the problem? (verses 38-40, summarize briefly)

    b. How was it was resolved? (verse 41)

4. a. Read 2 Kings 4:42-44. What was the problem? (verses 42-43a)

    b. How was it was resolved? (verses 43b-44)

5. Personal: Describe a time when God did something out of the ordinary for you or for someone you know.

Fourth Day:

And God's miracles and grace continue through Elisha.

1. a. Read 1 Kings 5:1-14. Who had a problem, and what was it? (verse 1)

   b. How was it was resolved? (verses 2-14, summarize briefly)

2. Challenge: Read 2 Kings 5:15-27. Why do you think Gehazi received such a harsh judgment?

3. Read 2 Kings 6:1-7. Briefly describe the problem and how it was resolved.

4. a. Read 2 Kings 6:8-23. What was Elisha's situation, and why was his servant fearful? (verses 8-15, summarize briefly)

   b. Why wasn't Elisha fearful? (verses 16-17)

   c. To whom was Elisha able to show mercy? (verses 18-23a, summarize briefly)

   d. What was the result? (verse 23b)

5. Personal: Are you facing some seemingly insurmountable problem or some unendurable fear? God has not changed. He is here for you in the midst of your difficulty and fear. Which miracle that you've read about in this lesson has most encouraged you and how?

Fifth Day:

God's long patience with Israel was at last exhausted. The Assyrians invaded and besieged the capital city of Samaria, and the Israelites were deported to Assyria.

1. Read 2 Kings 17:7-18. Why did God allow this to happen? (summarize briefly)

2. While wickedness increased in Israel, some changes were taking place in Judah—at least temporarily. Read 2 Chronicles 24:1-2, 17-19, 24, and compare the earlier and later periods of the reign of Joash of Judah.

3. Less than ten years after the deportation of Israel, Hezekiah became king of Judah. Briefly describe his character and his reign from 2 Chronicles 29:1-2; 30:1, 12, 26; and 31:1.

4. Personal: Throughout these books we have seen that those who served the Lord encouraged those under their authority or influence to also serve Him. Those kings who walked in unrighteousness and worshipped other gods paved the way for their entire nation to follow in their ungodly ways. Think of those in the sphere of your influence. Are you encouraging them to know, love, and serve the Lord, or are you paving the way for them to walk in unrighteousness? List some actions you could take to encourage them in righteousness.

Sixth Day:

Judah again fell into sin, yet one more revival took place there under the leadership of King Josiah.

1. Read 2 Chronicles 34:1-8, and briefly describe Josiah and his reign.

2. Read 2 Chronicles 34:14-21. What was discovered as they repaired the temple, and what was Josiah's reaction to it?

3. What pronouncement did God make through Huldah the prophetess in 2 Chronicles 34:24-28?

4. a. Just as God had warned, judgment came upon Judah and Jerusalem after the death of Josiah. Read 2 Chronicles 36:15-21 and briefly describe what happened. (verses 17-20)

    b. Why had this happened? (verses 15-16)

    c. How long would this judgment last? (verse 21)

5. God did not abandon His people forever. From 2 Chronicles 36:22-23, what did God cause to happen?

6. Personal: As you see, God is not playing. He gave both Israel and Judah many opportunities to repent. When they didn't repent, eventually judgment came. Yet even in judgment, His grace was extended to those who belonged to Him and put their trust in Him. If you have not yet turned from your sin and accepted Jesus Christ as your Savior, won't you do it now? Or perhaps you have accepted Christ but have slipped into sin. Won't you turn from that sin and ask God for forgiveness? Second Corinthians 6:2 tells us, "For he says, 'In the time of my favor I heard you, and in the day of salvation I helped you.' I tell you, now is the time of God's favor, now is the day of salvation."

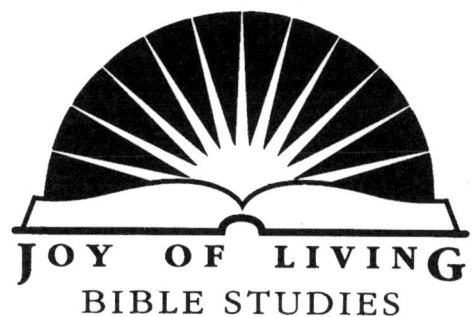

JOY OF LIVING
BIBLE STUDIES

2 Kings & 2 Chronicles 21-36 — Light and Shadow

Second Kings continues the record of the kings of Judah and Israel,[1] resuming the account of Ahaziah of Israel that started in 1 Kings. Ahaziah, who "provoked the LORD...to anger, just as his father [Ahab] had done" (1 Kings 22:53), fell through the lattice of his upper room and, while lying injured, sent messengers to consult the god Baal-Zebub as to whether he would recover. The angel of the Lord sent the prophet Elijah to meet the king's messengers, and through them severely rebuked the king and informed him that he would die.

When the king sent a band of fifty soldiers to capture him, Elijah called down fire from heaven to consume them. Another band of fifty men met with the same fate, and when the third band of fifty came, the captain begged Elijah to spare him and his men. The prophet went with him to the king to personally convey his sentence of doom. When Ahaziah died, his brother Joram succeeded him.

Elisha Inherits Elijah's Ministry (2 Kings 2-3)

The Lord miraculously took Elijah to heaven. Elisha was promised a double portion of Elijah's spirit, and this gift was evident in the first incidents of his ministry. First, by God's power, Elisha made bad water become wholesome in Jericho. Then, when some youths jeered at him along the road to Bethel, insulting him as a prophet of God, two bears mauled those who jeered as a judgment on their unbelief.

Moab rebelled against Israel's control, and Joram of Israel was joined by Jehoshaphat of Judah and by the king of Edom to suppress the rebellion. The allied kings found themselves in the desert with no water. They sought the counsel of Elisha, who sought the Lord only because Jehoshaphat was with them. He told them that God said the valley would be filled with water, though no rain would fall, and that their attack upon Moab would be successful. Evidently a flash flood did indeed fill the valley with water without any rain falling on the spot, and their campaign was successful as the prophet had predicted.

Mercy and Judgment (2 Kings 4-8)

Next a series of incidents from the ministry of Elisha are presented to indicate the ministry of mercy extended to individuals even while the judgments of God brought about the ultimate overthrow and exile of the nation of Israel. By the Lord's power, Elisha...

- provided a continuous flow of oil to a poor widow until she had enough to pay her debts;
- healed the barrenness of a wealthy woman of Shunem who had been kind to him; she bore a son, and he raised this same child from the dead when he succumbed to a sudden fever;
- rendered harmless a pot of poisonous vegetables;
- fed several hundred men with only 20 loaves of bread;
- healed the Aramean general, Naaman, from leprosy;
- caused a lost iron axe-head to float on top of water;
- opened his servant's eyes to see the Lord's chariots of fire that were protecting them from the Aramean army's siege;
- rescued the city of Samaria by making the attacking Aramean army hear sounds of a great army which frightened them away;
- predicted to Hazael, the Aramean general, that Ben-Hadad, king of Aram, would recover from his sickness but would be murdered by Hazael, who would then bring much distress upon Israel. This insight caused Elisha to weep, much as centuries later Jesus wept over the coming destruction of Jerusalem.

Then the writer returns to the history of Judah, giving a brief account of the reign of Jehoram, son of Jehoshaphat, who married the daughter of Ahab of Israel and "walked in the ways of the kings of Israel, as the house of Ahab had done" (2 Kings 8:18). As a result of Jehoram's evil ways, Edom revolted against the rule of Judah, as did the city of Libnah. Jehoram was succeeded by his son Ahaziah, who joined with King Joram of Israel to war against Hazael, king of Aram.

Judgment on the House of Ahab (2 Kings 9-10)

During the battle, Joram of Israel was wounded and returned to Jezreel to recover. While Ahaziah of Judah was visiting Joram in Jezreel, Elisha sent a prophet to anoint Jehu, the general of Israel's army, to be king in Joram's place, and to instruct Jehu to destroy the house of Ahab. Immediately Jehu headed for Jezreel. Learning that Jehu was on his way, Joram and Ahaziah set out to meet him, and came upon him at the vineyard that formerly belonged to Naboth. There the prophecy of Elijah to Ahab was fulfilled when Jehu killed Joram. As Ahaziah fled, he was wounded by Jehu's men and fled to Megiddo, where he died. Coming to Jezreel, Jehu saw Jezebel looking at him from her window. Jehu called to her attendants to throw her down, which they did, and her body was eaten by dogs, again according to Elijah's prophecy.

Jehu then became a terrible scourge in the hands of God. But he himself did not turn from the sins of Jeroboam and "was not careful to keep the law of the LORD...with all his heart" (2 Kings 10:31). As a consequence, parts of Israel fell into the hands of Aram. After a reign of 28 years Jehu died, and his son Jehoahaz reigned in his stead.

King Joash of Judah (2 Kings 11-12)

When the queen mother Athaliah (daughter of Ahab and Jezebel) learned that her son Ahaziah was dead, she seized the throne of Judah for herself, murdering the entire royal family (her own grandsons), except for an infant named Joash, who was hidden by his aunt Jehosheba in the temple. For the six years of her reign Athaliah did her best to introduce the worship of Baal to Judah. During this period Joash remained hidden in the temple. But in the seventh year, Jehoiada the priest, the husband of Jehosheba, organized a plot to put Joash on the throne. With the support of the army and the priesthood, he brought the seven-year-old boy out and publicly anointed him as king. Athaliah was killed, and the temple of Baal was destroyed.

Joash reigned for 40 years, and "did what was right in the eyes of the LORD all the years Jehoiada the priest instructed him" (2 Kings 12:2). The major event of his reign was the repairing of the temple. This was accomplished by special offerings which the king himself oversaw. The close of his reign was shadowed by an invasion from Aram, which Joash, in cowardice, averted by surrendering the treasures of the temple to the king of Aram. Soon after this Joash was assasinated, and his son Amaziah ascended the throne.

Continued Evil in Israel (2 Kings 13-14)

Jehoahaz, son of Jehu, came to the throne of Israel. He continued the evil of the kings before him, and in consequence the Arameans reconquered great portions of Israel. He then turned to the Lord and sought His help, and in response, a deliverer was granted to Israel. After a reign of 17 years Jehoahaz died, and his son Jehoash reigned. During his reign Elisha died and was buried, but even after his death miracles occurred. A group of Israelites seeking to bury a man's body were suddenly surprised by a band of raiders. They threw the body into Elisha's tomb, and when the body touched the bones of Elisha, the man sprang back to life. Thus, the final miracle relating to Elisha pictures the Spirit of Christ bringing life out of death.

Turning briefly to Judah, we are told that Amaziah, son of Joash, "did what was right in the eyes of the LORD, but not as his father David had done" (2 Kings 14:3). The high places were not removed, and worship continued there instead of at the temple in Jerusalem where it belonged. Amaziah won a great victory over Edom, and emboldened by this, he challenged the power of King Jehoash of Israel. They met in battle, and Amaziah was captured, a portion of the wall of Jerusalem was broken down, and the temple was entered and sacked. Though Amaziah reigned 15 years after the death of Jehoash, eventually a conspiracy was mounted against him, and he was killed. His son Azariah, only 16 years old, was made king of Judah in his place.

In Israel Jeroboam II, who followed his father Jehoash to the throne, reigned for 41 years. He reconquered all of Israel's territory from Aram. The prophets Jonah, Amos, Hosea, and Isaiah ministered in Israel during his reign. Despite this gracious touch from God, he walked in evil ways. After his reign his son Zechariah succeeded him.

Pride, Chaos, and Desecration (2 Kings 15-16)

Azariah, king of Judah, is known as Uzziah in both 2 Chronicles 26 and Isaiah 6:1. It was during his long reign of 52 years that Isaiah began his ministry. Azariah followed in the footsteps of his father Amaziah, but like him did not remove the high places nor interfere with the worship that went on there. In 2 Chronicles 26:16 we are told, "After Uzziah became powerful, his pride led to his downfall," and he sought to offer incense in the temple. For this he was stricken with leprosy, and remained a leper until his death. His son Jotham shared the regency with him and succeeded to the throne upon Azariah's death.

Meanwhile in Israel, things were rapidly sliding into chaos. Zechariah, son of Jeroboam, reigned only for six months and was killed by Shallum, who thus ended the dynasty of Jehu in the fourth generation as had been predicted. Shallum was on the throne only one month, and was succeeded by Menahem, who killed him and reigned for ten evil years, characterized by cruelty and extortion. During his days the land was invaded by the new world power of Assyria. Menahem was forced to pay tribute to Pul, also known as Tiglath-Pileser. Menahem was succeeded by his son Pekahiah, who reigned for two brief, evil years, and was killed by Pekah. During Pekah's reign of 20 years, Tiglath-pileser of Assyria invaded the northern portion of Israel and carried off captives from Galilee. Pekah later was killed by Hoshea. This murderous state of affairs in Israel was testimony to the persistent evil of king and people in turning from the living God.

Things were not much better in Judah. Though Jotham, son of Azariah, walked before the Lord in some degree of righteousness, during his 16-year reign both Aram and Israel threatened Judah, sent by the Lord as a judgment against her. Jotham was followed by his son Ahaz, who also reigned for 16 years. During his reign the nation sank to a new low, for Ahaz practiced the abominations of the Canaanites, even offering his son as a burnt offering. When the combined armies of Aram and Israel came against him, he sought help from Assyria, offering to be its vassal. He constructed a pagan altar in the temple, commanded the priests to offer sacrifices on it, and desecrated some of the holy furnishings. Yet during his reign, the prophets Isaiah and Micah carried on a faithful ministry of testimony to the truth.

Judgment Falls on Israel (2 Kings 17)

God's long patience with Israel was at last exhausted. During the nine-year reign of Hoshea, the last king of Israel, Assyria invaded and besieged Samaria. After three years the city fell, and the Israelites were deported to Assyria. The writer carefully assessed the reasons for this overthrow of the people of God. He contrasted their persistent sins of pride, evil practices, and idolatry with the patient love of God, who had warned them repeatedly through prophets and seers.

When the ten Israelite tribes had been removed, the Assyrian king repopulated the land of Israel with people from Babylon and other countries, who brought with them their own idols. They blamed their difficulties in the land on their ignorance of the God of Israel, and the king sent one of the deported priests from Samaria back to live in Israel and teach the newcomers about Him. Yet, 2 Kings 17:41 says, "Even while these people were worshipping the LORD, they were serving their idols." This religious mixture contributed to the enmity between Jews and Samaritans which, centuries later, was recorded in John 4.

Hezekiah of Judah (2 Kings 18-20)

While Israel was collapsing, Hezekiah, son of Ahaz, began his reign in Jerusalem. His father had been an ungodly king, but Hezekiah, perhaps warned by the fate of Israel, began to walk wholeheartedly before the Lord. It was said of him, "There was no one like him among all the kings of Judah, either before him or after him" (2 Kings 18:5). His first act, as we learn from 2 Chronicles 29, was to cleanse the temple. It took the Levites 16 days to carry out all the rubbish. Hezekiah also reinstated the Passover and destroyed the bronze snake Moses had made, which the people had been worshipping. Though God had used it for their blessing when Moses erected it in the desert, it had become a source of idolatry, just as many things which once blessed our lives become idols if we hold them in too high regard.

When Hezekiah had ruled for 14 years, Assyria invaded and took all of Judah's fortified cities. Frightened, Hezekiah offered to pay tribute, and was forced to strip the gold from the temple to make the payment. Undeterred, the Assyrians besieged Jerusalem. With arrogance, the Assyrian field commander challenged not only the might of Israel, but also the power of their God to deliver them. In desperation, Hezekiah turned to Isaiah the prophet, who reassured him that God was in control and would send the Assyrians back to their own country.

The siege was diverted by the report of an attack by Egypt. Before the field commander left, he sent a letter to Hezekiah, saying that they would return, and that nothing could save Judah from them. Hezekiah spread the letter before the Lord in the temple, and called upon God for deliverance. When the Assyrians returned, Isaiah sent word to Hezekiah announcing that the Lord held Assyria in utter contempt, and by His own mighty hand would turn them back. That very night an angel of the Lord entered the camp of Assyria and killed 185,000 men. Secular history records this as a great plague which swept the camp. With the remnant of his army, the king of Assyria departed.

When Hezekiah fell sick and was told he would die, he wept bitterly and begged the Lord for a reprieve. In response, his life was extended for 15 years, and as a sign to Hezekiah, the shadow on the sundial went back ten steps. In those 15 years, however, Hezekiah had a son named Manasseh, who became the worst king Judah ever had. His 55 year reign was the longest of any of the kings. Some have said, therefore, that Hezekiah was "the man who lived too long," for had he accepted the word of the Lord about his death, Israel would have been spared the terrible days of Manasseh. Also during these 15 years, Hezekiah received the envoys of the king of Babylon, and showed to them all the treasures of the house of the Lord. For this he was severely rebuked by Isaiah, who prophesied that the things which the envoys had seen would ultimately be carried to Babylon.

One Last Reformation (2 Kings 21-23)

Manassah's son Amon reigned for two years. He was killed in a conspiracy, and his son Josiah was eight years old when he came

to the throne. His reign marked the last attempted reformation before Judah was carried into captivity. When Josiah began to repair the temple, the Book of the Law was found. When this book was read to the king he was greatly distressed, and he turned for counsel to the prophetess Huldah. She responded that it was too late to save the nation from its fate, but that the king's reforms would delay the judgment of God until he had gone to his grave.

Josiah read the book of the Law to the people and then made a covenant to walk before the Lord and keep His commandments. The temple was cleansed of all articles of idolatry, and throughout the country idolatrous priests and altars were removed. The reform extended even to Bethel, which had been part of Israel, and the altar there which Jeroboam had erected was torn down and ground to dust. But despite King Josiah's sincere efforts at reform, the heart of the people was not truly repentant, and when Josiah was killed in a battle with Egypt and his son Jehoahaz succeeded him, the nation immediately returned to evil ways.

Judah Overthrown (2 Kings 24-25)

After Jehoahaz had reigned only three months, the king of Egypt deposed him and set his brother Eliakim, whose name he changed to Jehoiakim, upon the throne. For 11 years Jehoiakim reigned, first paying tribute to Egypt, and then for his last three years paying tribute to Nebuchadnezzar, king of Babylon. During these years the land was attacked by raiding bands, for the long patience of God was now ended.

Jehoiakim was succeeded by his son Jehoiachin, but after he had reigned only three months, Nebuchadnezzar overthrew Jerusalem and carried off to Babylon both the people and the treasures of the city. Jehoiachin was carried to Babylon as well, and his brother Zedekiah was set upon the throne as a vassal king in Jerusalem. In his ninth year he attempted to rebel against Babylon, and again Nebuchadnezzar besieged Jerusalem. In Zedekiah's eleventh year he was captured, blinded, and sent to Babylon in chains. The temple was burned, and the walls of the city were broken down. For 23 years the prophet Jeremiah had warned them that judgment would come if they failed to repent—that they would be taken captive by Babylon and remain there for 70 years.

The book of 1-2 Kings began with the wonderful scene of Solomon, his kingdom at peace, kneeling in his royal robes, praying to the God of heaven. Contrast this with the final scene when the temple lay in ruins, the city was destroyed, and the people were exiles in a foreign country. In this contrast we have a vivid picture of what happens in the human heart when it disobeys God. God's loving warnings are ignored for so long that God's patience draws to an end, and disaster follows.

Second Chronicles 21-36

Second Chronicles 21-36 covers the same events that we have just covered in 2 Kings, but gives more understanding of the reason events occurred. We learn from Chronicles that Manasseh, the most wicked king of Judah, after he had been taken captive by the Assyrians and sent to Babylon, repented from his evil and turned with a whole heart to God. He was restored to his throne, and in the closing years of his life accomplished certain reforms in Jerusalem. Though the king's repentance was genuine and met with the gracious restoration of God, his long years of evil had so affected the people that when his son Amon came to the throne, evil ways broke out in full force again. Then in 2 Chronicles 36:21 it is brought to our attention that for the 70 years of Judah's exile in Babylon the land enjoyed its sabbath rest, which the nation for 490 years had failed to keep.

An additional note of hope is struck at the very end of Chronicles. After the years of exile, the Lord moved the heart of Cyrus, king of Persia, to issue a decree to rebuild the temple in Jerusalem. This lays the groundwork for the record in the books of Ezra and Nehemiah.

The Path to Destruction

As we contemplate in these historical books the sorrowful record of the decline of the nation from its days of glory in the time of Solomon to the awful record of the exile, there are many valuable lessons to draw in the parallel experiences of our individual lives. Certain steps can be traced in the downward path of the nation.

First, there was the self-indulgence of Solomon, which weakened the spiritual strength of the people and caused the division of the nation under his son. Then his son Rehoboam "abandoned the law of the Lord" (2 Chronicles 12:1). As a result, the kingdom was invaded by the Egyptians. So in our own lives, when we turn away from obedience to the voice of God, our defenses are weakened and enemies begin to invade. When Jehoram ascended the throne of Judah, a spirit of jealousy entered the royal family, and he killed all of his brothers. Further, he led the people into unfaithfulness to God. This too was quickly followed by invasion and by disease. In Israel, King Ahaz introduced the worship of the Baals and burned his sons as offerings; immediately invasion followed.

We sometimes wonder why we fall prey to afflictions and oppressions. Often it is because the defenses of our soul are weakened by some inner idolatry. We find ourselves defenseless against the invaders of the spirit that bring on depression, frustration, and defeat. Yet just as God patiently tried to awaken the consciences of evil kings and to correct the practices of a stubborn and rebellious people, he reaches out in love to us through His Word and through His Spirit within us.

The Grace of God

By contrast, the good kings of Judah reflect the grace of God in cleansing and restoring the land and the people. There are five great reformations recorded during which God sought to arrest the deterioration of the nation and restore it to a place of glory and blessing.

Obey the Lord. The first reformation was under Asa. He not only removed the foreign altars and high places, but also "commanded Judah to seek the Lord, the God of their fathers, and to obey his laws and commands" (2 Chronicles 14:4). It is not surprising, therefore, that when he was attacked by the Cushites with a vast army, the prophet Azariah met him and said to him, "The Lord is with you when you are with him" (2 Chronicles 15:2). When we renew our determination to walk with the Lord, He will strike down our enemies and give us rest.

Study and Teach God's Word. Jehoshaphat also cleaned out the idols from the land, and in 2 Chronicles 17:7-9 a second principle of restoration is stated: "He sent his officials…to teach in the towns of Judah…taking with them the Book of the Law of the Lord."

Make Restitution. Joash restored the temple, and to do it he required the collection of long neglected taxes. The temple represents the human spirit, and the repairing and restoring of it is a picture of the strengthening of the spirit. This is often accomplished by the process of restitution—the paying of that which we owe. It may be an apology to someone, or the restoration of something wrongfully taken or used.

Renew Our Minds with Truth. In Hezekiah's reign, the temple was finally cleansed after 16 days of clearing out rubbish. Worship was restored, and the Passover celebrated. This pictures the cleansing of our spirit by putting away the filth which has accumulated, turning away from wrong ideas and attitudes, and turning back to the worship of the Lord and to the renewing of our minds with truth.

Hear and Walk Daily by God's Word. Josiah's restoration of the temple resulted in finding the Book of the Law which had been lost. Josiah himself publically read this book to the people and made a covenant to walk before the Lord and obey His commandments.

A Warning for Us

As we read these books we must bear in mind the words of Paul in 1 Corinthians 10:11: "These things happened to [Israel] as examples and were written down as warnings for us." From the beginning, even under David, there was a division within Israel, for he was king over only Judah for seven years, and after that over all twelve tribes. Though there was a division, all were intended to worship only at Jerusalem and to be under the authority of only one king. The heart of the nation was in the temple in Jerusalem where God dwelt.

Like Israel, our humanity is also divided, between the outer person, consisting of the body, and the inner person, consisting of soul and spirit. Within the soul—so closely linked with it that only the Word of God can divide between soul and spirit (see Hebrews 4:12)—is the spirit, the dwelling place of God. In this picture, then, the ten tribes of the north represent our human body, while the two tribes of Judah and Benjamin in the south represent our soul. Linked to our soul is the temple of our spirit where the Spirit of God Himself dwells.

When the nation began to disintegrate, it was the ten tribes of the north which fell apart first. It is amazing how early marks of sin begin to appear in the body when there is a dissolute and debauched way of life. The body is the first to deteriorate, as the northern kingdom of Israel was the first to decline. Judah—depicting the soul—was next to decline, slowed by the reformations we have noted. Ultimately, Judah too was carried away into captivity. For a few years the temple remained in Jerusalem, but in the end it too was stripped and burned.

Thus the whole record is a picture of a wasted life. It is the picture of an individual who is a Christian but who has built upon the foundation of Christ with only wood, hay and stubble (see 1 Corinthians 3:10-15). Eventually the test of fire comes, and only that which cannot be burned survives.

Study Questions

Before you begin your study this week:

- ❧ Pray and ask God to speak to you through His Holy Spirit.
- ❧ Use only the Bible for your answers.
- ❧ Write down your answers and the verses you used.
- ❧ Answer the "Challenge" questions if you have the time and want to do them.
- ❧ Share your answers to the "Personal" questions with the class only if you want to share them.

First Day: Read the Commentary on 2 Kings and 2 Chronicles 21-36.

1. What meaningful or new thought did you find in the Commentary on 2 Kings and 2 Chronicles 21-36, or from your teacher's lecture? What personal application did you choose to apply to your life?

2. Look for a verse in the lesson to memorize this week. Write it down, carry it with you, tack it to your bulletin board, on the dashboard of your car, etc. Make a real effort to learn the verse and its "address" (reference of where it is found in the Bible).

3. This week's questions focus on Ezra, Nehemiah, and Esther. If you have time, you may want to read through these books this week. As you answer the questions, you will be looking up passages of Scripture from various places in the Bible. This will help you discover that God's Word is a "whole," and that His message to us is the same from Genesis to Revelation.

The books of Ezra and Nehemiah are one book in the Hebrew Bible. They tell the story of the return of the people of God, after their 70-year captivity in Babylon, to the land of Israel; the restoration of the temple in Jerusalem; and the rebuilding of the wall around Jerusalem under Nehemiah's leadership.[1] The events of the book of Esther took place during the time of Jewish captivity in Babylon.

- ❧ 539 BC—The first Jews returned to Jerusalem from Babylon.   Cyrus is king.
- ❧ 516 BC —The temple is restored.   Darius is king.
- ❧ 479 BC —Esther, wife of Xerxes, became queen of Persia.   Xerxes is king.
- ❧ 458 BC —Ezra led the second expedition from Babylon.   Artaxerxes is king.
- ❧ 445 BC —Nehemiah rebuilt the wall of Jerusalem.   Artaxerxes is king.

Second Day:

The book of Ezra begins with the decree of Cyrus, king of Persia, giving permission to the Jews to return to Jerusalem and rebuild the temple of God.[2]

1. Read Ezra 1:1-3. Why did Cyrus make the proclamation? Who was permitted to go to Jerusalem, and what were they to do?

2. From the lists in Ezra 2 and later in Nehemiah, no more than 50,000 Jews under the leadership of Zerubbabel made this 700-mile journey.[3] Read Ezra 3:2-3. After they arrived in Jerusalem, what is the first thing they rebuild, and why? How did they feel about the people around them who had been inhabiting the land while they had been in exile?

3. a. Read Ezra 3:8-13. When did they begin rebuilding the temple? What was the people's response when the foundation was laid?

   b. Challenge: Why do you believe the older ones reacted as they did?

---

1. *What the Bible Is All About Bible Handbook*, p.170.
2. Two hundred years prior to this, Isaiah prophesied that a king named Cyrus would do this (see Isaiah 44:28—45:4). Before the fall of Jerusalem, Jeremiah prophesied the 70-year Babylonian captivity (see Jeremiah 25:1-12; 29:10).
3. At this time the Israelites are called Jews because most of them were of the tribe of Judah, hence the name "Jews."

4. Opposition toward the restoration of the temple developed almost immediately. Read Ezra 4:1-3. How did the enemies of Judah first attempt to interfere with the building of the temple? How did the leaders of Judah respond?

5. Read Ezra 4:4-8, 11-16. When compromise didn't succeed, how did the enemies of Judah attempt to stop the rebuilding of the temple?

6. Personal: The enemy of our souls will do anything he can to keep us from building a relationship with the Lord. What difficulties have you run into when you attempt to pray, to read God's Word, and to walk in obedience to Him?

Third Day:

Over 40 years had passed since Cyrus issued the decree for the Jews to rebuild the temple, and Artaxerxes was now king.[1]

1. Read Ezra 4:17-24. How did Artaxerxes respond to the accusations from the enemies of the Jews? What was the result? (Summarize.)

2. This discouraged the people, and they turned instead to building their own homes with many luxuries and comforts (see Haggai 1:1-4). God sent two prophets, Haggai and Zechariah, who turned the people back to their work on the temple. Then the enemies of Judah wrote a letter to Darius, the king, in an effort to stop the work. How did God turn to good what the enemy meant for evil in Ezra 6:1-14? (Summarize briefly.)

3. About 60 years after the temple was completed, Ezra led another group of Jews back to Jerusalem. Read Ezra 7. Who was Ezra (verses 1-6, 10), and what was he to do (verses 14-20, 25-27)? (Summarize briefly.)

4. When Ezra and the others arrived in Jerusalem, they found that the Jews and the Levites who had earlier returned to the land had again begun to intermarry with the people who inhabited the land. From Deuteronomy 7:3-4, what had God said about this and why?

5. Personal: Ezra and the heads of the families took steps to deal with the problem quickly. As believers, we are to guard ourselves from any type of compromising relationship. Have you ever been in or are you now in any type of relationship (dating, close friendship, business partnership, etc.) with someone who leads you away from the Lord? What did you do about it, or what will you do about it?

Fourth Day:

As the book of Ezra recounts the rebuilding of the temple, so the book of Nehemiah tells of the rebuilding of the walls of Jerusalem. Nehemiah opens almost 75 years after the temple was completed and 13 years after Ezra arrived and began teaching God's Word. Nehemiah held a position of honor as cupbearer to King Artaxerxes.

1. a. Read Nehemiah 2:1-8. After receiving a report concerning the ruin of Jerusalem, Nehemiah wept, fasted, and prayed for several days. What request did Nehemiah make of the king? (verses 5,7-8)

---

1. The chronology of the kings of Persia mentioned in the book of Ezra is confusing. It appears that the information in Ezra chapters 4-6 is grouped according to theme rather than by chronology. For example, Ezra 4:6-23 serves as a parenthetical comment. It would have been natural for the writer of the book of Ezra to follow a discussion of the problems related to rebuilding the Jerusalem temple (4:1-5) with information on a similar resistance the Jews encountered while rebuilding the walls of Jerusalem (4:6-23). (Eric Lyons, "Kingly Chronology in the Book of Ezra," Apologetics Press, 2005, http://www.apologeticspress.org)

   b. What was the king's response? Why did he grant Nehemiah's request? (verses 6, 8b)

2. Sanballat the Horonite and Tobiah the Ammonite official were powerful men in the Trans-Euphrates area. From Nehemiah 2:10 and 4:1-3, how did Sanballat and Tobiah feel, first about the arrival of Nehemiah to Jerusalem, and then about the rebuilding of Jerusalem's wall?

3. a. Read Nehemiah 4:7-23. When their taunts and mocking didn't stop the Jews from rebuilding the wall, how did the enemy attempt to stop them? (verses 7-8, 10-12, summarize briefly)

   b. How did the Jews respond? (verses 9, 13-23, summarize briefly)

4. Read Nehemiah 6:15-16. How long did it take them to rebuild the walls? How did the Jews' enemies and the surrounding nations feel about this, and why?

5. After this, in a great gathering of the people, the Book of the Law of Moses was read and explained to them. Read Nehemiah 8:9-12. The people were convicted of their sin to the point of weeping. How were they comforted? Why did they have great joy? (Summarize briefly.)

6. Personal: Do you rejoice when you begin to understand what God's Word says? What is your response when it convicts you of sin? Write 1 John 1:9, personalizing it by inserting your name. Does this make you rejoice?

Fifth Day:

The book of Esther tells of an incident that occurred during the Jewish captivity in Babylon. Although God is not mentioned in the book, throughout it we will see the unseen hand of God moving and working providentially, as He so frequently does in all our lives.

1. Read Esther 1:1-9. Xerxes was the great king of Persia. Briefly describe the three banquets, their lavishness, and the guests who attended each one.

2. When Xerxes' queen, Vashti, refused the king's summons to show herself at his banquet, she was deposed. After this (between Esther chapters 1 and 2), Xerxes made his historic attack on Greece with a huge army and suffered a terrible defeat in the famous naval battle of Salamis (480 BC).[1] Upon his return, another queen was sought for Xerxes. From Esther 2:2-4, briefly describe the search.

3. Read Esther 2:5-7. What do you learn about Mordecai and about Esther from these verses?

4. Read Esther 2:8-17. Because of her beauty, Esther was one of the young girls taken to the king's palace, where she would complete twelve months of beauty treatments before going to spend the night with the king. What do you learn about Hegai, about Mordecai, and about Esther from these verses?

---

1. *What the Bible Is All About Bible Handbook,* p.191.

5. Read Esther 2:19-23. What did Mordecai overhear, and what happened because of it?

6. Personal: Mordecai and Esther had found it necessary to hide their nationality. Esther's parents had died when she was younger; then she was torn from the home of Mordecai to become the concubine and possible wife of a man she didn't know. Sometimes the situations in life seem unfair, but God wants His children to trust Him in all situations, whether they seem fair or not. Are you in a difficult situation? Will you trust the Lord in the midst of it? Write 1 Thessalonians 5:18.

Sixth Day:

Haman was a descendant of King Agag of the Amalekites, long-time enemies of the Jews (see Deuteronomy 25:17-19). He was more powerful than the other nobles. All the royal officials at the king's gate knelt and paid honor to him—everyone except Mordecai.

1. a. Read Esther 3:5-14. How did Haman feel about Mordecai's action, and what did he do about it? Did the king believe him? (verses 5-11)

   b. What was Haman's final decree? (verse 13-14)

2. a. Read Esther 4:12-16. Mordecai called upon Esther to appeal to the king on behalf of the Jews, knowing that it could mean her death to go before him without being summoned. What harsh truth did Mordecai tell her in verses 12-14?

   b. Esther decided to appeal to her husband. What did Esther ask all the Jews in Susa to do for her prior to going before him, and what was her attitude? (verses 15-16)

3. a. Read Esther 5:14—6:11. The king welcomed Esther and accepted an invitation to have dinner with her and to bring Haman with him. Although Haman rejoiced over this, his rage increased against Mordecai every time he saw him. What did Haman's wife suggest? (5:14)

   b. How did Mordecai's earlier good deed benefit him? (6:1-3)

   c. How did Haman's arrogance backfire on him? (6:4-11, summarize briefly)

4. a. Read Esther 7:1—8:11. At a dinner with the king and Haman, Esther revealed who she was, who Mordecai was, and how Haman had plotted to destroy the Jews. What was Haman's final end? (7:10)

   b. Did Xerxes stop the destruction of the Jews? (8:3-8,11)

5. Read Esther 10:1-3. God had caused Esther to become the queen. What became of Mordecai?

6. Personal: You never know what God is doing in our lives. He wants us just to live and walk in obedience with Him, trusting Him to guide us and use us. Will you trust that His hand is at work in your life through every situation that comes your way, whether you see it in a miraculous way or not? Trust that, if you are willing, He will use you wherever you find yourself. Write Proverbs 16:9, personalizing it by inserting your name.

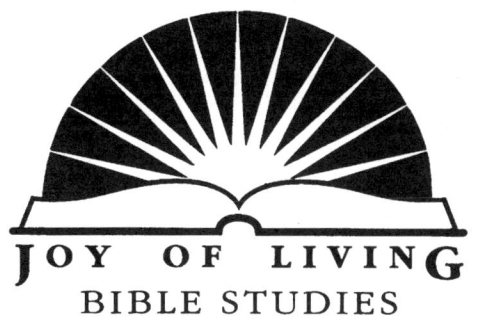
Ezra, Nehemiah & Esther — The Way Back[1]

The books of Ezra and Nehemiah, which are one book in the Hebrew Bible, tell the story of the return of the people of God to the land of Israel in 539 BC after their 70-year captivity in Babylon, the restoration of the temple in Jerusalem in 516 BC, and the rebuilding of the wall around Jerusalem under Nehemiah's leadership in 445 BC.[2] The events of the book of Esther took place during the time of Jewish captivity in Babylon.

The Book of Ezra

The book of Ezra begins with the same words which close the book of 2 Chronicles. They recount the decree of Cyrus, king of Persia, directing exiled Jews to return to Jerusalem in order to rebuild and restore the temple of the Lord. This gives us our clue to the meaning of Ezra, for it is a book which recounts the method of God in restoring a heart which has fallen into sin.

The book covers the ministries of two men: Zerubbabel and Ezra. Both of these men led expeditions of Jewish exiles back to Jerusalem from Babylon. Zerubbabel was a descendant of David, and thus of the kingly line. Ezra descended from Aaron, and was therefore a priest. This suggests that in the work of restoration both a king and a priest are needed. The work of the king is to build, or in this case, to rebuild. The work of the priest is to cleanse.

Restoration in an individual life always requires these two ministries. There is need to rebuild the character through a recognition of the kingship and lordship of Jesus Christ in the human spirit. Such building involves the recognition of God's right to own and direct us and to change us according to His will. But restoration also involves cleansing. The spirit and the soul are to be cleansed by our great High Priest, who is able to wash away our guilt and restore us to a place of fellowship and blessedness before God.

The Ministry of Zerubbabel (Ezra 1-6)

Under Zerubbabel an early return took place. This kingly descendant led about 50,000 people from Babylon back to Jerusalem. Cyrus, king of Persia, may have known of Isaiah's predictions concerning his instrumentality in the hands of God (see Isaiah 44:28; 45:1), for he

gave willing aid to the Jews who returned, giving them the articles from the temple that Nebuchadnezzar had carried off.

Arriving in Jerusalem in the seventh month of the year, they celebrated the Feast of Tabernacles. This was the time when Israel lived in tents to remind them of their pilgrim character. This feast also looks forward to the eventual regathering of Israel from their worldwide dispersion to celebrate the reign of Messiah upon the earth in great power and glory (see Zechariah 14:16-21).

The list of those who returned, given in Ezra 2, indicates that not only did various families and clans go back, but also a company of priests, a smaller number of Levites, certain servants who were to assist the Levites in their service, and a number of people whose genealogy was somewhat uncertain.

Their first corporate act was to build an altar on the original temple site, in the midst of the ruins. Under the open sky they erected an altar to God and began to worship and offer sacrifices, as the Law of Moses commanded. This pictures the first act of a heart that desires to return from wandering in darkness and the ways of the world to real fellowship with God. The altar involves sacrifice, worship, and praise. The sacrifice is that of our right to run our own lives; the worship is the enjoyment of a restored relationship, where our hearts are ministered to by the only One who can fully meet our needs; and the praise is that of a rejoicing heart.

Next they laid the foundation of the temple. This work was met with mixed feelings. Some of the people shouted praise to the Lord, and others, including those who had seen the first temple built by Solomon, wept aloud. Perhaps you too have felt this way. Have you ever returned to God after a time of coldness and withdrawal, with a great sense of joy as the foundations of fellowship were re-laid by the Spirit, yet with regret for the loss of wasted years?

Opposition toward the restoration of the temple developed almost immediately. Here we see portrayed the force at work in every human heart which immediately rises up to oppose everything God attempts to do. There is a great lesson here in how this force reveals itself. The opposition first appears as friendly solicitude. The people of the land approached Zerubbabel and said, "Let us help you build because, like you, we seek your God and have been sacrificing to him since the time of Esarhaddon king of Assyria, who brought us here" (Ezra 4:2). This apparently friendly and openhearted desire to participate in the work marked a very subtle attack upon the returning exiles. It is not difficult

---

1. This is an overview. You can study Nehemiah and Esther in more detail in the Joy of Living studies titled *Nehemiah* and *Esther.*
2. *What the Bible Is All About Bible Handbook*, p170.

to say "no" to an enemy who breathes fiery threats of slaughter, but when he offers to help with your project, it is difficult to say "no."

Zerubbabel declined their offer of help and stated the Jews would do the work alone. It may have seemed a bit churlish, but God had commanded Israel to remain separate from other nations. The world tries to interject its concepts and methods into the lives of God's people, saying, "Advance yourself; do this for your own glory. Use religious ways to advance your own purposes, and thus win admiration, power, and fame," but God has made it clear that these are to be rejected.

When the offer of friendship was rejected, the people of the land began to mock the Jews, discouraging Israel from doing the work that God had commanded. These so-called "friends" even used legal means to undermine Israel's right to build, for they eventually obtained from Artaxerxes (a later king of Persia) a decree to stop the rebuilding of the temple in view of the rebellious history of the Jews. The work was stopped for a period of six years, and the temple lay silent with only its foundations completed. Those who return to fellowship with God may find that their past rises again to impede their progress, but a determination to go on with God will overcome even this handicap.

It was during this period that the people turned instead to building their own homes with many luxuries and comforts (see Haggai 1:4). God sent two prophets, Haggai and Zechariah, to turn the people back to their work on the temple. God also moved the heart of Darius (another king of Persia) to search for the original edict of Cyrus which allowed the restoration of the temple. When it was found, a decree was sent to Israel to permit the rebuilding to continue.

At last the work was finished, and the Passover was celebrated, marking the beginning of the Jews' new life under God. Since the Passover pictures the conversion of a Christian, we see that when we have been restored in the temple of our spirit to fellowship with the living God, we will delight in remembering and celebrating what God has done for us through His Son Jesus Christ.

The Ministry of Ezra (Ezra 7-10)

Ezra also led a band of exiles back to Jerusalem. It was said of him, "He was a teacher well versed in the Law of Moses, which the LORD, the God of Israel, had given. The king had granted him everything he asked, for the hand of the LORD his God was on him" (Ezra 7:6). What kind of a man was this, whom a Gentile king regarded so highly that he would give Ezra anything he asked? The secret is given in Ezra 7:10, "For Ezra had devoted himself to the study and observance of the Law of the LORD, and to teaching its decrees and laws in Israel." He was not only a Bible reader; he was also a Bible doer.

Ezra's specific assignment from the king was "to bring honor to the house of the LORD in Jerusalem" (Ezra 7:27). To achieve this, Ezra gathered leading men from Israel, including many Levites. After prayer and fasting they set out on their journey, committing themselves to the providence of God to keep them safe on their way. In due time they arrived in Jerusalem, and there Ezra found an incredible situation. The Jews and the Levites who had earlier returned to the land had again begun to marry with their ancient enemies, the Canaanites, Hittites, Perizzites, Jebusites, Ammonites, Moabites, Egyptians and Amorites.

Centuries before, God had given specific orders that the Israelites were not to intermingle with these tribes. Intermarrying had broken the strength of the nation, undermined the power of God among them, and finally separated them into two nations. At last, as they succumbed to the idolatry of those whom they had married, God delivered them into the hands of their captors. After 70 years of captivity they had not learned a thing. This is a vivid reminder that the sinful nature within us never changes. No matter how long we may walk in the Spirit, we will never arrive at a place where it is impossible to revert to the worst we have ever been, if we depart from dependence upon the Spirit of God.

When Ezra heard that the people had disobeyed God by intermarrying with the surrounding pagan peoples, he tore his garments, pulled hair from his head and beard, and sat down appalled until the evening sacrifice. But as the book nears its close, Ezra prayed to God and confessed this great sin of the people. In graciousness God moved the hearts of the people, and the leaders came to Ezra and acknowledged their wrong. A proclamation was issued, and the people assembled in front of the temple, confessed their guilt, and agreed to put away the wives and children they had acquired outside the will of God.

This does not mean that a Christian must put away his or her unbelieving spouse today, for this is symbolic teaching. It means that we are to put away whatever comes from the sinful nature. Thus the work of Ezra was completed, and the task to which he had been assigned—that of bringing honor to the temple—went forward.

The Book of Nehemiah

As the book of Ezra recounts the building of the temple, so the book of Nehemiah tells of the rebuilding of the walls of Jerusalem. The order is significant, for the way back to God after a period of decline and captivity to evil must always begin within our spirit—our temple. But the next step is to begin a reconstruction of the walls—the defenses of the spiritual life—to protect against the attacks of any enemy.

Rebuilding the Defenses

Nehemiah received a report in the citadel of Susa concerning the ruin of Jerusalem. When he heard it he wept for several days, fasting and praying before God. Thus the first step in rebuilding the defenses of any life is to become greatly concerned about the ruins. Have you ever taken a good look at the ruins of your life? Have you looked at the possibilities that God gave you and seen how far you have deviated from that potential? If you will begin to be concerned and weep over those ruins, you will have begun the process of rebuilding.

This mourning was followed by confession. Nehemiah prayed and acknowledged the sin of his people and the justice of God in having fulfilled the words of Moses, given in warning centuries before. Also in Moses' words, recorded in Deuteronomy, was the promise that when anyone, even in a distant country, would begin to pray to God, a recovery and restoration to the place of blessing would begin.

The prayer of confession was followed by commitment. A plan was already forming in Nehemiah's mind even while he had been in prayer. He had something definite which he wanted to ask, and he prayed that God would grant him favor in the presence of the king. Invariably there are factors over which we have no control and God must arrange them. When, in his work as cupbearer, he next came before the king, Nehemiah's face showed concern over the city of his fathers. At the king's request Nehemiah told him what was troubling him.

Rebuilding the defenses of a city, or of a life, requires courage to face the opposition that immediately arises. Encouraged by the king, Nehemiah returned to Jerusalem, where he found certain Canaanite leaders who were greatly displeased that someone had come to promote the welfare of the Israelites. Whenever a believer says, "I will arise and build," Satan always answers, "Then I will arise and oppose."

To face such opposition requires not only courage, but also caution. Nehemiah rode out around the city of Jerusalem by night, surveying the ruins of the wall and taking note of what needed to be done. He made an honest survey of the facts and then began to lay his plans.

Principles of Reconstruction

If the walls of your life are broken down, so that the enemy is getting at you and you easily fall prey to temptation, pay attention to the principles of reconstruction set forth in Nehemiah 3. We learn, first of all, that the people were willing to work, and second, that they became personally involved and began right where they were. Each one began to work on the part of the wall that was nearest to his house, and so called forth the deepest of personal involvement on his part.

The reconstruction of the walls centered about the 10 gates of the city. The names of these gates, in the order in which they appear, is most instructive.

The Sheep Gate. Through this gate sacrificial animals were brought into the city to be offered on the altar. This clearly pictures the Lamb of God, whose blood was shed on the cross for us. The cross is always the starting place to regain strength in your life. You must recognize anew that the work of the cross is to put to death that which is for your own glory and advancement.

The Fish Gate. Jesus said to His disciples, "Come, follow me… and I will make you fishers of men" (Mark 1:17). This gate pictures the witness of a Christian. If you never give an account of what the Lord has done for you, then the Fish Gate needs to be rebuilt.

The Jeshanah Gate—literally, "the Old Gate." This gate represents the unchangeable truth of God upon which everything new must rest. In many places today the old truth is being forsaken, but if you allow the old truth to go, you will find that the wall crumbles, and enemies outside gain access to your soul.

The Valley Gate. This suggests the place of humility. On almost every page of Scripture God speaks against human pride. He looks always for the humble, the contrite, and those who have learned that they are not indispensable. We need to be reminded that "God opposes the proud but gives grace to the humble" (James. 4:6).

The Dung Gate. This represents an essential process in life: you need to eliminate that which is corrupt and defiling. No life can be strong or healthy that does not have an often-used elimination gate.

The Fountain Gate. Jesus said to the woman at the well: "The water I give [you] will become in [you] a spring [fountain] of water welling up to eternal life" (John 4:14). This speaks of the Holy Spirit, who is to be like a river of life within you, enabling you to obey God's will and His Word. To drink from that flowing fountain is to be refreshed in spirit, and to find power to do what God requires.

The Water Gate. Water is always, in Scripture, the symbol of the Word of God. The interesting thing about the Water Gate was that it did not need to be repaired. Thus the Word of God never breaks down, nor does it need repair, it simply needs to be used again.

The East Gate. Facing the rising sun, this is the gate of hope. It anticipates that which is yet to come, when the trials of life end, and the glorious new sun rises on the day of God. This gate needs to be rebuilt in many of us who fall under the pessimistic spirit of this age and are crushed by the hopelessness of our times.

The Horse Gate. The horse in Scripture is the symbol of warfare, that is, the need to do battle against the forces of darkness. This gate, too, is often in need of repair. As the apostle Paul said, "For our struggle is not against flesh and blood, but against the rulers, against the authorities, against the powers of this dark world and against the spiritual forces of evil in the heavenly realms" (Ephesians 6:12).

The Inspection Gate. This speaks of our need to take a good look at ourselves now and then and evaluate what we are doing.

The final verse of Nehemiah 3 brings us around again to the Sheep Gate, the gate of the cross. The cross must be at the beginning and end of every life.

Pray and Watch

The derision of Jerusalem's Canaanite neighbors continued to mount, and threats were made against the lives of Nehemiah and other leaders. In response, Nehemiah went to prayer and set up a guard. From then on, the workers labored with their weapons beside them, keeping watch and building at the same time. Nehemiah's enemies tried various approaches to stop the work, but he focused on the work to which God had called him. The end result was the finishing of the wall and the gaining of the respect of surrounding nations when they saw the hand of God at work.

The time came to reaffirm the spiritual strength of the nation. In a great gathering of the people, the Book of the Law of Moses was read to them anew, accompanied by exposition given by Ezra. When the people were convicted by the reading of the law to the point of weeping, Ezra and Nehemiah comforted them with reassurances that the Lord had made provision for their forgiveness, and that "the joy of the LORD is your strength" (Nehemiah 8:10).

Nehemiah 11 recognizes gifts among the people—Levites, gatekeepers, singers and other ministries. This is similar to the New Testament, which sets the church to discover and put to work the gifts of the Spirit that are given among them. In Nehemiah 12 is the story of the dedication of the wall. The people gathered and marched around the wall with instruments, singing and shouting, playing and rejoicing.

During the reading of the law, it was learned again that the people of God should give no official place to either an Ammonite or a Moabite. Nehemiah, who had gone back to Persia and apparently had returned to Jerusalem for the dedication of the walls, reminded the high priest that Tobiah was an Ammonite, yet he had been given a place to live within the very temple itself. This is the Tobiah who had done so much to hinder the work of building the wall. To correct this, Nehemiah went in and threw Tobiah's household goods out into the street.

Further, Nehemiah found that the priests and Levites had been cheated, so he restored the money that belonged to them. Then, discovering that the people were violating the Sabbath, he commanded that the city gates should be shut when the Sabbath began and kept shut until it was ended. Finally, Nehemiah dealt again with the problem of intermarrying with forbidden people groups. When he learned that one of the priests was the son-in-law of Sanballat, who had done so much to oppose Nehemiah's work, he chased the young man from his presence.

To us it may appear that Nehemiah was overly severe in dealing with these violations, but here is a man who has learned that there can be no compromise with evil. He manifests one of the greatest lessons the Spirit of God can ever teach us: to say "no" when it needs to be said, and to say it with firmness and determination. Those who have made a mark for God throughout the history of the church have been those who have learned to say "no" at the right times.

The book of Nehemiah demonstrates how to rebuild the walls of strength in our individual lives, and how to maintain those walls by unceasing resistance to allurements and attacks which attempt to force us to compromise. How important it is to be ruthless against the forces that undermine and sap the vitality of our lives in Christ.

The Book of Esther

The book of Esther tells of an historical incident that occurred during the Jewish captivity in Babylon. It doesn't appear to be a religious book, because nowhere does the name of God appear—nor any mention of heaven or hell. However, within Esther we see the unseen hand of God moving and working providentially, as He so frequently does in all our lives. As in our study of other Old Testament events, we can see in the account of Esther the spiritual parallel to humanity itself. This pattern appears in the tabernacle, in the temple, in the division of the nation of Israel, and now in the book of Esther.

Xerxes, the king, depicts the human soul, comprising mind, emotions and, especially, will. His capital city, Susa, pictures the body, in which all his decisions and actions will be most immediately felt. His empire is the sphere of influence which each one of us exerts on all whom we contact. The queen, bound in marriage to the king, depicts the human spirit, the place of fellowship, refreshment and communion with God, which is intimately related to our soul.

Xerxes's empire was in a time of peace. No enemy threatened his kingdom from the outside; there was nothing to do but display the lavish glory of his kingdom. Adam before his fall, was just such a king.

His whole empire, the Garden of Eden, lay at rest, and he was free to do nothing more than manifest the riches, fruitfulness, and glory of his kingdom while enjoying unhindered communion with God.

During a six-month long feast, which began in joy and merrymaking but ended in tragedy, Xerxes was lifted up in pride and sought to disgrace his queen. Her refusal to submit to his demands resulted in her being deposed from the throne. This decree became a law which could not be changed. When Adam chose to assert the desire of his will over what he knew in his heart that God wanted, he laid the groundwork for the eventual fall of the entire race. His disobedience caused him and all his descendants to enter a fallen state, losing communion with God, which they were helpless to change.

In his loneliness, Xerxes sought a new queen. He chose Esther, one of the Jewish captives, who had been raised by and therefore was under the control of her cousin Mordecai. In the spiritual parallel of our lives, fallen humanity, in loneliness and restlessness, also searches for a new place of communion and fellowship with God, even though we ourselves hardly know what we are looking for. The new queen depicts our moment of conversion. At this moment we receive a new spirit which, though we do not yet understand it, is under control of another—the Holy Spirit. Throughout this book, Mordecai is seen to be the power behind the throne, thus depicting the humility and self-effacement of the Spirit of Christ.

When Haman, a descendant of Amalek—who always pictures the sinful nature—convinced Xerxes to decree that the Jews should be destroyed, Esther risked her life to save her people. She told the king that his decree would mean her death as well as her people's death. The king, in consternation, had Haman hanged, and Mordecai was exalted to a place of power. Another decree by the king removed the threat of death from the Jewish captives and allowed them to kill their enemies in self-defense. We see this picture fulfilled in Romans 8:2, where Paul tells us that "through Christ Jesus the law of the Spirit of life [sets us] free from the law of sin and death."

In Esther we have the same king and the same kingdom at the end as we do at the beginning. The only difference is that Haman is out and Mordecai is in. But what a difference! Just as the king and kingdom remain the same, so the Christian remains the same person when the Spirit is given the place of control in his life. Personality does not change, but it is cleansed and enhanced by the presence of the Spirit. So Paul can say, "I have been crucified with Christ and I no longer live, but Christ lives in me" (Galatians 2:20).

Summary

Throughout this study of Old Testament History we have seen that trusting and obeying God is the way to blessing and fellowship with Him, while disobedience brings His judgment. Yet, even in the midst of judgment, God provides a way for forgiveness and is working both outwardly and behind the scenes to bring about repentance and draw those that belong to Him, back to Himself.